Families, Alcoholism, & Recovery

Celia Dulfano

Foreword by
Daniel J. Anderson

Families,
Alcoholism,
&
Recovery

Revised Edition

Jossey-Bass Publishers · San Francisco

Originally published as *Families, Alcoholism, and Recovery: Ten Stories.*
© 1982 Hazelden Foundation.

Copyright © 1992 by Jossey-Bass Inc., Publishers, 350 Sansome Street,
San Francisco, California 94104. Copyright under International, Pan
American, and Universal Copyright Conventions. All rights reserved.
No part of this book may be reproduced in any form—except for brief
quotation (not to exceed 1,000 words) in a review or professional
work—without permission in writing from the publishers.

For sales outside the United States, contact Maxwell Macmillan
International Publishing Group, 866 Third Avenue, New York,
New York 10022.

Manufactured in the United States of America.

The paper used in this book is acid-free and meets the
State of California requirements for recycled paper
(50 percent recycled waste, including 10 percent
postconsumer waste), which are the strictest guidelines
for recycled paper currently in use in the United States.

10% POST
CONSUMER
WASTE

Library of Congress Cataloging-in-Publication Data

Dulfano, Celia.
    Families, alcoholism, and recovery / Celia Dulfano. — Rev. ed.
      p. cm. — (The Jossey-Bass social and behavioral science
series)
    Includes bibliographical references and index.
    ISBN 1-55542-484-8
    1. Alcoholics—United States—Family relationships.
2. Alcoholics—Rehabilitation—United States. I. Title.
II. Series.
HV5132.D86 1992
362.29'23'0973—dc20
                                    92-19299
                                      CIP

REVISED EDITION
HB Printing   10 9 8 7 6 5 4 3 2 1   *Code 9284*

Contents

ix

**Part Three:
Women, Family Therapy, and Alcoholism**

Foreword

In the relatively brief history of the treatment of alcoholism as a facet of health care, the concept of providing specialized services for the families of alcoholics has an even briefer history. In recent years, we in the field of alcoholism treatment have acknowledged the fact that the family of the alcoholic frequently does need specialized assistance. In her original book, Celia Dulfano, a pioneer in the study of the impact of alcoholism on the family, demonstrated how family interactions and family systems affect the recovery from alcoholism for the entire family. In this new updated and expanded work, she continues to advance our knowledge of alcoholism and family therapy with additional case presentations and concepts reflecting the growing maturity of the family systems model of therapeutic intervention.

This book will be especially helpful for any professional working in the alcoholism family treatment field. But it will also be suitable for any family member who is living with a practicing or recovering alcoholic.

The case presentations are practical, real-life situations illustrating a variety of ways of focusing on some of the major issues that must be dealt with by families affected by alcoholism.

By using simple and realistic examples based on years of clinical experience, Dulfano illustrates a multitude of creative pathways through the interactive maze of family relationships.

Her ability to describe this systems model in simple, straight-forward language also communicates a new sense of hope for all of us working with or living with someone with an alcohol problem.

July 1992   Daniel J. Anderson
President Emeritus
Hazelden Foundation
Center City, Minnesota

Preface

Alcoholism affects both sexes, all age groups, and all bands of the socioeconomic and cultural strata of the United States and other industrialized nations. The magnitude of its effects mandates a better understanding of the problems of alcoholism and better therapeutic approaches. We need clearer blueprints for ameliorating its effects, and much clearer guidelines for prevention and early intervention.

For many years, the helping professions overfocused on the individual alcoholic. Stopping the abuse of alcohol was obviously a priority, but alcoholism's impact on the life of the family and other significant units was all but ignored. It took time and experience to teach us that we must reach further, beyond the individual alcoholic, out to the other people affected by the illness: the alcoholic's spouse, parents, children, and co-workers. But even when the mental health field began to find the "other victims" around the alcoholic, agencies and organizations, having little or no idea of how to use this expanded view in practice, continued to touch them only peripherally.

As the eye-opening experience of treating alcoholic families became more common, we learned that we needed far more information than was then available. I was probably among the first of the practitioners who began to reach out to other professionals with the message from Alcoholics Anonymous (AA) and Al-Anon that alcoholism affects all family members. In 1982, with the first edition of this book, I tried to reach a mixed audience of professionals and interested laypeople. At that time, much of the treatment of alcoholics was being done by counselors, most of whom were themselves recovering alcoholics. Almost no relevant literature and research were available. Thus this book grew out of my early attempts, in the late sixties and early seventies, to conduct workshops and seminars to train agencies, professionals, and students to look at alcoholism in a new way — as a disease affecting an entire network of people.

New directions broadened the treatment system. A wider community orientation developed, as did more comprehensive treatment of the individual alcoholic. But to ensure continued progress, community and voluntary organizations, government agencies, treatment providers, and other interested parties must take appropriate and concerted action.

Audience

I hope to contribute to the solution of this problem by presenting in this book a simplified clinical approach to family treatment of alcoholism. It is directed to several groups of professionals in the helping field, including therapists, counselors, social workers, nurses, and other health and mental health providers. All of these professionals deal at some time with interpersonal conflicts created or compounded by alcoholism. Students in training for these professions will also benefit from the information here. Perhaps this book will awaken in them the optimism that comes from realizing that successful therapeutic outcomes are very possible.

This book can also be used, as it was very successfully in its first edition, during training sessions, meetings, and especially workshops. It provides material for discussions and amplification of the cases and situations, thus offering the opportunity to hear new or different approaches.

I also hope that in the general public the many families affected by alcoholism but hiding it will find information, solace, and hope in the examples portrayed.

Because this book was designed to offer a clinical approach to a variety of health care professionals, I have deliberately touched only peripherally on the theoretical background and the research in the field. However, the interested reader will find most of the recent significant literature on the theoretical framework for family therapy in the treatment of alcoholism discussed in various chapters and listed in the suggested readings in the back of the book.

The first part of this book offers a simplified theoretical framework for approaching the problems created by alcoholism. The case presentations that follow analyze the most common clinical situations and offer specific therapeutic guidelines. The stories, culled from my own experience as teacher, therapist, and supervisor, allow practitioners a wide look at the problems and therapeutic approaches that depend on the agencies involved, and the problems of nonalcoholic members of families affected by alcoholism in their milieu. The cases are told as stories, in down-to-earth language, so that any reader, professional or lay, can understand the devastation engendered by alcoholism in a given situation. Names and family circumstances have been changed in every case to protect individuals' privacy.

Throughout the text, whenever I do not refer to a specific person, I alternately use the pronouns *he* and *she* to avoid sexism.

The book emphasizes the techniques of removing alcoholism as the "core family problem" and reestablishing it as the problem and responsibility of the individual alcoholic member. In families in which alcoholism has created a bizarre structure, methods of stimulating individual family members to resume their specific responsibilities are illustrated. When alcoholism becomes a family's core problem, it stunts the family's normal functioning and growth. Family members tend to assume makeshift roles, disrupting, compounding, and confusing the system. From a therapeutic point of view, removal of the alcoholism as the shared problem can free the individuals to look at their own behavior and to try to correct it.

Since the original edition first appeared, additional problems related to the alcoholic family have been recognized in the field. The revised edition includes issues related to violence, sexual abuse, and incest and their long-term effects on children growing up in such families; such issues were known but largely ignored in the past.

Part One emphasizes the value of family treatment. Chapter One discusses the necessity of expanding the focus of treatment to encompass the family members of the alcoholic. The family offspring, ignored for many years, are now recognized as a legitimate focus of treatment and concern. Chapter Two uses a case example to portray the development of alcoholism in a family and to show how it affects the emotional life of the family members. A discussion of an appropriate therapeutic intervention follows.

Part Two uses case examples to illustrate typical situations that crop up in treatment. Chapter Three shows how helping an alcoholic individual attain sobriety is not enough if distorted family patterns are left untreated. Chapter Four illustrates the alcoholic's mechanism of denial and perception that it is others who need the help. It shows how this mechanism can bring the alcoholic to therapy. Chapter Five shows a case where family therapy proved unsuitable and individual therapy continued as the treatment of choice. Chapter Six presents a case of family collusion to hide the problem of the alcoholic family member. Uncovering and confronting the alcoholism in such a case may require a massive family intervention and can precipitate a family crisis. Chapter Seven discusses the danger of focusing on a child's problems when the real problem is an alcoholic parent. Chapter Eight deals with family patterns that develop around an alcoholic member's incapacity. These patterns may continue to hamper individual and family development even after the alcoholic has achieved sobriety. Chapter Nine discusses the problems particular to low-income families, who have to cope with poverty and discrimination in addition to the problems posed by alcoholism. Chapter Ten deals with the problems of the long-term alcoholic, who requires rehabilitation in the form of group therapy and often housing. Chapter Eleven presents the case of the unreachable alcoholic, whose family members need to be freed from the effects of alcoholism on their lives. A change in the life of the family will usually, to some extent, reach the alcoholic. Chapter Twelve describes the alcoholic who recovers but is impeded by the alcoholism of another family member. To be effective, treatment has to include the whole family.

Part Three deals with tailoring family therapy to alcoholic families. In Chapter Thirteen the reader will find an example of the multimodal psychotherapy technique applied to a group of daughters and wives of alcoholics who were treated in a combined group therapy and family therapy mode. In this situation, when problems related to the participants' families of origin surfaced, separate family sessions were conducted. These sessions allowed the individual to contribute her experience to the group in resolving personal conflict within her own family. The net result was a useful therapeutic combination of family and group therapy. Chapter Fourteen includes a summary of the various therapeutic techniques discussed throughout the book. Tailoring family therapy to alcoholism requires determining the focus, assessment, and interventional techniques most appropriate for each case. These family stories, told in human fashion, reflect the real life of families affected by alcoholism.

Newton, Massachusetts   Celia Dulfano
July 1992

Acknowledgments

This book grew out of my experiences of over thirty years working in the alcoholism treatment field. During that time, I had contact with many families, professionals, and students. I want to thank all of them for contributing to my growth as a person and as a therapist.

My special gratitude goes to the late Gladys M. Price, who introduced me to the field of alcoholism therapy at the Washingtonian Hospital in Boston in 1961. She was my mentor, colleague, and friend for many years.

I was fortunate to have the skillful editorial help of Fran Hitchcock in the first edition. For this edition I want to express my thanks for the encouragement and guidance of Rebecca McGovern. Xenia Lisanevich did a superb job in editing the final manuscript.

My heartfelt thanks go to my husband for his caring and assistance throughout the years and to my two daughters, who patiently accepted my professional forays out of the home.

C. D.

To my husband, Mauricio J.,
my daughters, Guila and Shevy,
their husbands, David and Ben,
and their offspring,
Asaph, Yael, Shoshi, and Maia

The Author

Celia Dulfano is a lecturer at the Boston University School of Social Work. She is also a consultant in private practice in Newton, Massachusetts, and conducts seminars and workshops around the country and abroad. She received her teaching degree from the Teachers College, Cordoba, Argentina, and her B.A. degree (1942) from Cordoba University School of Law. She received her M.S.W. degree (1962) from the Boston University School of Social Work. Dulfano has been on the faculty of the State University of New York, Brooklyn, and the Rutgers University Summer School of Alcoholism. In 1991, she received the Boston University Alumni Award for Outstanding Contributions to the Field of Social Work.

Dulfano has devoted most of her professional years to the teaching, training, and practice of family therapy in alcoholism. She has played a leading role on many professional boards dealing with training and services in the alcoholism field and has held memberships in many professional societies. She is the author of six chapters in books on alcoholism and family therapy, including *Practical Approaches to Alcoholism Psychotherapy* (1985, edited by Zimberg and others), *Group Process Today: Evaluation & Perspective* (1974, edited by Milman and others), and *Alcoholism in the Jewish Community* (1980, edited by Blaine).

She has always been involved with new ideas and experiences. She came from the Argentine hinterlands to become a teacher and to study law. In 1948, she was among the first to volunteer to go to Israel, where she taught new immigrants, created a model nursery school, and worked as a youth examiner for the Department of Justice, assessing cases of sexually abused children.

After Dulfano came to Boston, through her field work for the School of Social Work at the Washingtonian Hospital she made her first contact with her lifelong interest — the problem of alcoholism. Later she consolidated her training in family therapy at the Maimonides Community Mental Health Center in Brooklyn and then as a senior clinician at Roosevelt Hospital in New York. From 1970 to 1977, she was director of the New York State Department of Mental Hygiene's Social Work Training Program in Alcoholism, which included Columbia, Syracuse, and Hunter College schools of social work.

Families,
Alcoholism,
&
Recovery

Part 1

Alcoholism and Family Systems

1

Expanding the Focus of Treatment

When Peter Richardson was ten, his school referred him to the pediatric department of the community hospital. Peter's teachers complained that he was impossible to reach. He was always either withdrawn and daydreaming or disrupting the class with nervous activity that he seemed totally unable to control. He also presented severe reading problems. With these symptoms, the obvious course was to have Peter evaluated by a child psychiatrist. The diagnosis was early schizophrenia.

Peter began individual treatment and remedial reading classes. But both therapists noticed a curious inconsistency. Sometimes Peter came on time for his appointments, related well, and worked hard on his reading assignments. Sometimes he showed up half an hour late with a vague excuse and repeated the daydreaming and/or hyperactivity reported by the school.

A hospital social worker made an appointment to see Peter's mother, Collette. As they shook hands, she smelled liquor on Collette's breath, at 11 A.M. The social worker asked Collette whether she had been drinking. Surprised, Collette confided that she had had to have a drink before coming to keep the appointment.

As we learned more about the Richardson family, we discovered that both Collette and Sean, Peter's stepfather, were alcoholics. Sean was a steady drinker, but Collette was only intermittently drunk. While sober, she functioned capably as a working mother, supervising Peter's activities, sending him to appointments on time, and in general giving him some sense of stability. But when Collette, too, was drinking, Peter went home to a deserted apartment or to parents who were drunk or had passed out. He stayed in the apartment, watching TV, caring for his dog, who was his closest companion, making himself a sandwich for dinner, and whenever necessary phoning the local liquor store for a delivery. His "early schizophrenic" behavior was the behavior of a child deprived of his parents by the disease of alcoholism.

This is a book about real people, with their desires and sufferings. They all are different, and the selection of cases is not arbitrary. The case histories come from my own practice and illustrate different alcoholism problems and therapeutic solutions. The affected people came into contact with various professional disciplines through a variety of agencies — agencies that did not always identify alcoholism as the primary problem.

These families all have been profoundly affected by alcoholism. But they are also the Harrisons, the O'Briens, and the Stewarts. I have always felt very uncomfortable about labeling patients. The helping professions, it seems to me, are overused to stereotyping. We even tend to take historical data from the standpoint of an already imposed diagnosis. The diagnosis is alcoholism; therefore the person behind the diagnosis recedes. This happens to an even greater extent to the families of alcoholics. The alcoholic's spouse is not seen as a person. He or she is not even a patient — only the patient's spouse.

In emphasizing the problem, the human individualism of the people described is lost. Yet too much specificity is not useful; an exact report of the treatment of Family Y by Therapist X would be useful only to the clones of the Ys and Therapist X, and then only for a short period of time. In writing these case reports, I have tried to steer a course between the two extremes, presenting material that is specific enough to be human yet generalized enough to be useful. If the reader arrives at an understanding of how to look at alcoholism in the family and learns to approach the family as a unit for therapy, the book will have accomplished most of its goals. What is proposed is an extension of rather than a replacement for what exists.

Theory Versus Practice: Transition

As the study by the Institute of Medicine (1990) reported, the alcoholism treatment field seems always to be in a transitional stage due to its complexity. The historical record is still brief, and we see significant changes occurring. People seeking help at present often receive effective assistance. Much has been accomplished. Even so, no one focus of treatment is likely to be effective for all people. The principal task is to provide the most effective treatment for a *given person* with a *given problem.*

We still tend to zero in on the individual alcoholic, as we have always done. At the same time, it is common knowledge (as it has always been) that alcoholism is a social syndrome. Alcohol is a drug. Abuse of alcohol is an illness. But it is an illness that is deeply interconnected with the current context of the individual's life. Most therapies recognize this, however implicitly. Many therapies involve removing the patient from this context, either in theory or in fact, while therapy is in process.

The development of what have been called ecological therapies over the past several decades has given alcoholism therapy tools for approaching and dealing with the patient's environment. In theory, we can now work with both individuals and "significant others" in a multieffort attack on both the intrapsychic and the interpersonal components of the alcoholism syndrome. Unfortunately this theoretical knowledge has not yet been incorporated into our actual therapeutic structures. Alcoholics in treatment often go from agency to agency, from therapeutic method to therapeutic method. They receive intense input into personal change and growth but get little help for the actual problems of coping with an unchanged interpersonal context, let alone help in ameliorating that context.

The focus of treatment must be expanded. While we continue to be concerned for the individual alcoholic, we must also address the vast and heterogenous spectrum of problems that are no less important and severe.

Working with alcoholism in the family is a particularly effective therapeutic method in many cases. This significant interpersonal context can be changed in ways that support the maintenance of sobriety and the reintegration of the sober alcoholic as a coping and competent family member. Furthermore, it is common knowledge in the field that valuable preventive therapy can be done with people who have experienced the stresses of living with an alcoholic. To find it actually being done is still a rarity.

The problems created by alcoholism are complex, and to deal with them effectively may require a multifaceted leadership representing society as a whole.

The Alcoholism Therapist: Changes in Perspectives

As a therapist working with alcoholism in specialized agencies, mental health agencies, and the family therapy division of a psychiatric unit, I have experienced this transitional period in my own professional development. Like most professionals now specializing in alcoholism, I learned the dynamics of the syndrome by working with individual alcoholics. I became acquainted with the vast literature and research on the medical and psychological correlates of alcoholism. Like alcoholics themselves, I have had to learn that alcoholism is an illness, not a sin. Coming from a culture in which wine is customarily served with meals, I had to begin by accepting as part of my own personal beliefs the concepts of alcoholism as a disease and of alcohol as a drug.

As I worked with individual alcoholics, I became aware of the consequences of this problem for the alcoholic's family and social network. Over a period of time, I began to recognize that the focus on the individual alcoholic, while not incorrect, was incomplete. The theory underlying alcoholism therapy was that a vulnerable individual who had personal deficits probably combined with a physiological predisposition was escaping personal and social pressures by abusing alcohol. Great efforts therefore were put into helping the individual deal with those personal deficits. Sometimes he or she was hospitalized or institutionalized for medical treatment combined with psychotherapy or behavioral therapy. Sometimes the therapy of choice was group treatment or referral to a self-help organization like

Alcoholic Anonymous (AA). In either case, as the social worker and specialist in alcoholism therapy, I coordinated my efforts with the techniques of the psychotherapist, physician, psychologist, behavior therapist, or self-help organization to help the patient attain sobriety and develop new skills for the purpose of sustaining sobriety. The patient was then, in effect, returned to the environment in which the alcoholism had developed and was expected to maintain sobriety in the face of the unchanged pressures that had combined to exacerbate the problems in the first place.

As soon as the problem is conceptualized in these terms, an enhanced therapeutic strategy springs to mind. Would it be possible to attack the problems not only from the standpoint of the individual alcoholic but also from the standpoint of the interpersonal systems that correlate with the individual's problems? Might it be possible to change salient aspects of the social system?

Today it is accepted that individuals experience different problems related to their use or abuse of alcohol. More than one problem exists, as do different kinds of individuals. Different methods of treatment go beyond individual psychotherapy. Comprehensive rehabilitation programs that include alcohol education, alcoholism services, and family intervention in coordination with Al-Anon, Alateen, and many other services will help remove the problems that contribute to the continuation of the drinking.

Like their patients and like all other human beings, therapists are influenced by their own social networks: "significant others" in my network included family therapists, who helped me look at individual alcoholics in a new way. I began to apply their ideas to the study and treatment of alcoholism.

The effect of family therapy can be compared to the consequences of the discovery of the lever. On the one hand, it seems so simple as to be obvious: everybody knows that people affect each other. On the other hand, the consequences of using this knowledge are so far-reaching as to be almost incalculable. When the individual is seen actually interacting within significant social contexts, whole new aspects are opened not only to conceptualization but also to therapeutic change.

Salvador Minuchin (1969) describes the results of this change of perspective in his anecdote of John. The therapist who sees John, age fourteen, in the context of individual sessions hears the boy describing a relationship with his mother "which is ambivalent, but with a strong element of attraction." The boy hates his father. "The therapist unravels the history of this process and its repetitive nature throughout the development of the child. He is aware of the boy's anxiety and of his defensive patterns. He interprets the material as an Oedipal conflict with paratactic distortion of the present situation."

The context in which data are gathered shapes not only the data but also the way the therapist organizes the data. "The therapist who gathers his data in individual sessions will build up an explanation of John's behavior which includes his internalization of his parent figures, the historical development of his conflict with them and the apparently compulsive intrusion of this conflict into extrafamilial and seemingly unrelated situations in John's life."

But if the therapist sees this fourteen-year-old "Oedipus" with "Jocasta" and "Laius," a different picture emerges.

> In [family] interviews, the therapist sees that the relationship of John and Jocasta is characterized by intermingled closeness and hostility. During the sessions most of the communications John sends are directed towards his mother, and even when he does talk to Laius, his father, he seems to do so through his mother, who translates and explains her son to her husband.
>
> The relationship between the spouses is characterized by a lack of intimacy and by very poor communication. There is an absence of marital conflict; disagreements usually are side-tracked into the father's attacking his son for his misbehavior outside the family.

Now the therapist has more than additional data. He also has a new way of organizing data, one that suggests targets for change in the interpersonal process that is feeding into John's Oedipal conflict.

A similar change in perspective occurs when a therapist looks at an alcoholic in a family context. The rather vague recognition that context affects behavior is immediately replaced by the observation that the alcoholic is part of a significant social system, responding to it even as it responds to him or her. We now accept that alcoholic behavior is a product of factors. The medical aspects of alcoholism, the psychological components of addiction, and the personal deficits all are still part of the picture. But the picture is wider now. It is more complex, but it is also more accurate. The interpersonal transactions of alcoholic and spouse, parent, child, and sibling are now part of the "diagnosis." They are also part of the possibilities for therapy.

The field of alcoholism treatment has recognized that alcoholism is the product of three factors: the biological, the psychological, and the social. What we are doing now is beginning to learn about the "and." Working with families affected by alcoholism is one promising way of learning about that "and." The cases in this book are presented as data for those who want to explore these new directions.

Where Do We Stand Now?

The first steps are largely accomplished. Alcoholism is now generally recognized as an illness though occasional arguments are made against that premise. Educational efforts are bringing this knowledge to the public at large, though a great deal of work remains to be done in this area. Furthermore, our methods of treating the individual alcoholic have been improved and made more specific by medical and mental health research. Unfortunately we still tend to focus too narrowly on the individual alcoholic when it comes to therapy. As a result, the effectiveness of our interventions is undercut by the patient's natural environment.

This overfocus on the individual alcoholic has two other consequences as well. First, we are neglecting a large population in need of primary mental health care. Second and even worse, we are neglecting opportunities for badly needed preventive therapy.

The spouses, children, parents, and colleagues of the alcoholic are sometimes called the "other victims" of alcoholism. It would be more accurate to call them "participants" in the alcoholic syndrome, but whatever the label, they need our help. They include battered wives and children who live with an alcoholic whose frustration tolerance is low and whose behavior is implusive and inconsistent. They include children who grow up in families whose functioning is warped by the incapacity of one parent. They include the people undergoing the year-in and year-out stresses of compensating for an alcoholic: the husband trying to support the family and handle housework, child-rearing, and community contacts so well that no one begins to wonder about his wife's "migraine"; the co-workers who cover for good ol' Joe; the baby-sitter who will be driven home by a man who has had a few too many, and the driver who may meet them on the road.

Alcoholism is a chronic disease that typically takes ten to fifteen years to develop. By the time an alcoholic comes to therapy, therefore, his family, friends, and associates have been dealing with the impact of progressive alcoholism for years. The children may never have known adequate parenting. The spouse is by definition either overburdened or defeated. Yet even when their problems are recognized, the nonalcoholic members of these families are too often seen only as adjuncts to the major problem. Their own needs go unattended in the drive to treat the individual alcoholic.

It is little wonder that alcoholism seems to "run in families." Many experts have suggested some hereditary components to alcoholism, and some research supports this premise (Goodwin, 1973, 1976, 1979). But growing up with an alcoholic parent is quite sufficient to explain why children of alcoholics have difficulties and statistically often become alcoholics themselves. It is unnecessary to postulate a biological factor. The chaos in the alcoholic family, its instability, the lack of adequate role models—this is not the stuff of healthy childhood.

In the late 1960s, after many years of working in alcoholism therapy, Margaret Cork (1968) decided to explore the lives of children in alcoholic families. In her book *The Forgotten Children,* she wrote about interviews with over one hundred children. Her conclusion was a strong recommendation to pay attention not only to these children but also to the life of the family as a unit.

In the past few years, some studies of alcoholic families have been guided by the hypothesis that children of alcoholics learn to fulfill specific roles in the process of adjusting to the family environment (Wegscheider, 1980; Seixas & Youcha, 1985; and Black, 1982, among others). Children become the family hero, scapegoat, lost child, or mascot. This may be an aid to identity, but it can also become a problem if the roles become attached to personality traits and the individuals do not know how to change.

Forrest (1991) reports a "role slippage" in these families. Members move out of one role and into another. Such role reversal occurs constantly, resulting in major problems in the family. As a family therapist, however, I think *labeling* is too generic a concept to be useful. Individual alcoholics are different, as are alcoholic families. We have to look more thoroughly into other factors in the environment.

A new movement calling itself Adult Children of Alcoholics (ACOA) also seems to me to be handicapped by overgeneralization. The development of the alcoholic family is affected by the duration of the problem, the number of generations involved, access to treatment, recovery or continuing substance abuse, the presence of other medical and mental health problems, and a host of other family and individual problems, ranging in severity from predictable transitional difficulties to the extreme dysfunction of sexual or physical abuse. Also significant, as Beletsis and Brown (1981) point out, are the children's ages when alcoholism becomes a disturbing fact in the family; whether alcoholism affects the father, the mother, or both; the family's economic stability or lack of it; and the availability of support within the extended family and the family environment. No single picture can be drawn for the type and extent of alcoholism in a family, making it impossible to form open predictions about the outcome of affected family members.

The United States has an estimated ten million active alcoholics. We cannot even begin to estimate the number of people affected by these alcoholics. But we will meet some of them in the case examples in this book. How many women like Irene, growing up with an alcoholic parent, learn to see themselves not as people in their own right but as adjuncts to some man's problems? How many children like Joanne remain overinvolved in an alcoholic parent's life long after they should be making lives for themselves? How many boys like Marty Stewart, deprived of an effective male role model, find it difficult to cope with the world of peers? How many girls like Carmela Giacomelli run right home after school to baby-sit, fix snacks, and start dinner while Mama "naps" on the couch? And aside from the current pain of these situations, how many of these people are "disasters waiting for a place to happen"?

Compensation is possible. We can help these "other victims" develop their own lives as coping individuals and we can help the individual alcoholic. But then what happens to the family?

How can the individual integrate his or her own personal growth in the context of the family if we do not create changes in that context? By working with the individual alcoholic and the alcoholic family, we do both primary and preventive therapy. In many cases, we can break the patterns that otherwise would entrap this generation and be passed along to the next.

Basic Considerations for Treatment

The causes of alcoholism are multifaceted and deeply rooted. They are also not yet well understood. Nevertheless, alcoholism the disease can be combatted therapeutically without a complete understanding of its etiology. It is possible to design effective therapeutic approaches to alcoholism by defining it simply and pragmatically as both an illness that strikes an individual and a social syndrome that develops over time. In time, parents, spouse, children, extended family members in the alcoholic family, and colleagues and friends in the extrafamilial world all become part of this social syndrome. They in turn affect the alcoholic and his symptoms in a continuing process of interrelating feedback.

Therefore, except in the cases in which an alcoholic has become totally estranged from social networks, a therapist intervening with alcoholism in a person is intervening with a whole system of groups. The therapist may never see anyone else besides the individual alcoholic and may not even be aware of the people he or she is impacting, but the impact is there. Ideally the therapist should be aware of this network and interrelate with it. This will make the therapeutic process shorter and more effective, while also improving the chances for preventive therapy.

Though it is a chronic disease, alcoholism has acute phases, and it is often an acute crisis that brings the alcoholic to the attention of the therapist. The alcoholic has admitted herself to a detoxification unit or is committed for treatment by a family that has finally reached its limit. Less dramatically, therapy may commence because the alcoholic is threatened with divorce, loss of a job, or perhaps her own sense that her drinking has gone past her control. Sometimes the crisis may be caused by a therapist who recognizes the symptoms of hidden or unacknowledged alcoholism and confronts a patient with them. Therefore the chronic nature of the disease may not be obvious.

In most cases, the alcoholic has been in difficulty for years. Her functioning may have deteriorated steadily, or maybe long periods of stability have only occasionally been threatened by uncontrolled drinking. In either case, a whole life-style has evolved around this dysfunction, and probably a group of people — the patient and her network — exist whose interactions have been shaped by the problems of alcoholism.

Abundant research has established that biological, psychological, and social components all are present in the etiology of alcoholism. In any given case, these three factors intermesh in the development of the chronic syndrome.

Addictive Components

Alcohol is a depressive psychoactive drug. We tend not to recognize this fact because alcohol is used socially and is easily available in more places. Nevertheless, it is a drug, and physiological addiction can occur. Frequent ingestion of alcohol builds up tolerance to the drug, and gradually larger doses are needed to obtain the same results. The ingestion of continually larger doses bathes the tissues of the central nervous system in high concentrations of the drug, which results eventually in physical dependence. In other words, though alcoholism is a socio-psycho-physiological syndrome, some components are purely physiological. Emotional symptoms lead to the excessive drinking, but the increasing physiological dependence causes emotional reactions, increasing the rate of drug-seeking behavior on both levels. Without the individual's awareness, he or she becomes dependent on the drug. As tolerance builds, use of alcohol increases, and the craving and the need to continue drinking become an unrelenting drive.

Treatment of the physiological components of alcoholism depends very much on the stage of the illness. During its early stages, alcoholism is a symptom. The individual who is developing dependency on alcohol is drinking to relieve some underlying discomfort or to satisfy some underlying needs. The reasons for the drinking, whatever they may be, are the disease; abuse of alcohol is a symptom of that disease. As drinking progresses over the years, however, alcoholism itself becomes the disease. Whatever may have driven the individual to drink in the first place, the cyclic phenomena (tolerance — physiological dependency — loss of control and craving) begin to take their toll. At this point the individual is physically and psychologically addicted to alcohol.

In the early stages, the dynamics and clinical picture of alcoholism vary considerably with each patient and the individual circumstances. In the later stages, the physical, physiological, and social deterioration of the alcoholic become entirely too typical. By now, alcoholism is truly a disease with a single etiological agent — alcohol — and an essentially unified diagnosis.

A physician treating an alcoholic in the early stages must explore the individual's drinking carefully. Some patients may be able to stop drinking on their own. Withdrawal symptoms must be anticipated. A good history of the individual's drinking patterns will help the physician in making the decision whether hospitalization is necessary.

If reason is found to expect severe withdrawal symptoms ("the shakes" or even "the d.t.'s" — which appear after two to three days of withdrawing alcohol), the patient should be hospitalized for controlled detoxification with medication. Most units use a combination of drugs (tranquilizers, stimulants, and antidepressants) to try to decrease the severity of withdrawal symptoms. Ideally the dosage of medication is decreased until, in the last days of detoxification, the patient becomes drug free. Switching from alcohol addiction to other drug addictions and/or combining the two are unfortunately very common.

Antabuse (disulfiram) is often prescribed for patients who have completed detoxification. Antabuse blocks an enzyme that is necessary for the metabolizing of alcohol in the system, and as a result, the body is oversensitized to alcohol. Thus, when a patient who is taking Antabuse consumes alcohol, highly unpleasant symptoms will develop within a few hours. These may include a sudden drop in blood pressure, cold sweats, palpitations, difficult breathing, a racing pulse, severe headache, and/or reddened skin and bloodshot eyes. Taking a drink therefore is negatively reinforced: the alcoholic who is taking Antabuse knows that the consequences of taking a drink will be disagreeable. So he stays dry, no longer ingesting the drug to which he is physiologically and psychologically addicted. His functioning improves, if only because of the physiological benefits of sobriety.

Antabuse can be a valuable adjunct to alcoholism therapy. It is not, however, an effective therapeutic agent by itself. It also has side effects in some cases, which may include occasional headaches, skin allergy, fatigue, and loss of sexual potency. Still it can be useful for an alcoholic who genuinely wants to stop drinking but is uncertain of his ability to maintain sobriety. Ideally the patient will commit himself to taking

Antabuse and will follow through as part of the progress toward recovery.

Medical intervention can be a crucial part of the treatment of alcoholism, but it usually is not effective in itself. So far, no successful pharmacological treatment for alcoholism has been developed. Physiologically, "once an alcoholic, always an alcoholic" holds true. Research on the physiological components of alcoholism, including its possible hereditary factors, plus the anecdotal evidence of the many sobered alcoholics who thought that "just one" would not hurt, all indicate that a cluster of biological factors are only partially amenable to pharmacological therapy. If the social and psychological aspects of the alcoholism are successfully treated, however, the inherent physiological factors do not hamper attaining and maintaining sobriety, as long as the individual does not ingest alcohol.

It is generally agreed that the alcoholic suffers from personality deficits — or inadequate coping mechanisms — that predispose him or her to drink as a means of escaping or seeking gratification through intoxication. Therapy designed to ameliorate these deficits is generally a process of education — teaching the alcoholic to replace inadequate coping mechanisms with healthier ones. Beyond this agreement, as might be expected, views of alcoholism and its therapy vary according to the training of the therapist.

The psychodynamic analyst will see the alcoholic as an emotionally immature, passive, dependent individual with strong difficulties in relating meaningfully to others. Alcoholism is seen as a manifestation of neurosis based on deficient or arrested development of personality, rooted in childhood. Therapy will guide the patient to a search for the introjected experiences from the past that are governing his behavior in the present, interpreting them in a way that guides the patient toward remolding his life. The existential psychiatrist will work with the patient on developing alternative life-styles that are more gratifying.

The behaviorist will see alcoholism as a socially acquired, learned behavior maintained by numerous antecedent cues and consequent reinforcers that may be of a psychological, sociological, or physiological nature. Therapy will combine negative conditioning to drinking with positive conditioning to some alternative life-style.

The social psychiatrist will stress the impact of peer groups on individual behavior. The sociologist may cast the problem as almost entirely societal, requiring social changes, as does the activist who discusses "ghetto alcoholism."

Any modern etiology of alcoholism must take into account the pervasiveness of drinking in our social customs. Like the peyote of the Yaqui Indian, alcohol has formed part of humankind's social ritual since prehistory. A complicated ritual surrounding the use — and sometimes the abuse — of alcohol is common in human societies. Herodotus reported that one primitive people routinely debated any issue before the tribe first sober, then drunk. In 1895, in the sophistication of upper-class Edwardian England, the essayist Jerome K. Jerome remarked in *Idle Thoughts of an Idle Fellow,* "We are forever drinking on one excuse or another. A man never feels comfortable unless he has a glass before him. We drink before meals, and with meals, and after meals. We drink when we meet a friend, also when we part from a friend."

Recognition of the abuses of alcohol and concern with the relationship of alcoholism to poverty and human degradation led to an enormous investment in abolishing this drug during the nineteenth century. But the other side of the coin was also recognized.

In the twentieth century, our labeling of the social problems associated with alcoholism has changed and perhaps improved. The problems themselves have not. Treatment of alcoholism must all too often take into account the stresses of poverty, racism, unemployment and underemployment, and ethnic discrimination, even though alcoholism is far from confined to victims of such forces. Therapy will often involve shoring up depleted supportive systems in the face of difficulties human beings ought not to have to deal with. "Band-Aid therapy," the political activist sneers, and this charge is undoubtedly accurate. Nevertheless, in the continuing and marked absence of societal change, "Band-Aid therapy" can still foster change and improvement in the lives of some.

Alcoholism Therapy

It will be obvious that all the etiological ideas of alcoholism have some validity, more in some cases than in others, depending on circumstances. By the same token, therapies designed according to these ideas can be valid, more in some cases than in others, depending on circumstances. Some physiological factors render an alcoholic vulnerable to alcohol addiction. Alcoholism may well be related to childhood conflicts, and the tendency is to reconstruct past behavioral responses in different environments. Alcoholic behaviors are "learned" and can be negatively reinforced or extinguished. Social factors are significant, both the larger forces like poverty and racism and the more immediate network of interpersonal transactions in which the alcoholic lives his life. Behind alcoholism is a person, and every alcoholic, like every person, is different. In other words, alcoholism is the interaction of biological, psychological, and social factors. These factors combine differently and have different importance in the life of each individual patient.

The therapist working with alcoholism therefore should know as much as possible about alcoholism and its etiology and should take into account as many individual and social factors as possible when searching for points of therapeutic entry. Some form of individual or group therapy may be the treatment of choice in one case. In another, work with the problems of alcoholism may be handled by AA or other self-help groups while the therapist works with the sobering alcoholic and the family to build a new supportive network. In still another case, the therapist may have to help a family cope with the strains of living with an alcoholic who continues to drink. Close consultation with medical personnel may be indicated for a patient who is on Antabuse or other drugs. The more the therapist can deal with the biological, psychological, and social aspects of alcoholism, the more effective therapy can be.

Therapy with Families Affected by Alcoholism

We now turn to the main subject of this book—the discussion of therapy with families affected by alcoholism. Family therapy

is only one of many possible therapeutic strategies. Nevertheless it is often the most effective type of intervention for both
primary and preventive therapy. The family is the social unit
most easily available to the therapist. It is a highly significant,
perhaps the most significant, source of the positive and negative feedback that validates an individual's self-perception. An
alcoholic can maintain her self-perception while recovering with
the support of extrafamilial "significant others," such as a therapist or AA sponsor. But her self-perception while recovering
will be greatly enhanced if her competence is positively reinforced by her family group. Finally, the family is a significant
source of support to help the individual cope with the demands
and stresses of life.

Family therapy of alcoholism is a way of dealing with the
needs of the alcoholic in the context of dealing with a human
system. The goal of therapy is not only sobriety. The goal is
a changed family: a system in which human beings can support each other's competence.

The basis of family therapy is *systems theory*. This is a way
of looking at human beings that is at once familiar and yet
radically different. Systems theory is based on an observation
that humans undoubtedly made in the cave: people affect each
other. If I got caught in a traffic jam on my way into town this
morning and I snarl at your sunny "Good morning," my annoyance will diminish your cheer, just as your cheer will dim-
ish my annoyance. As human beings, we know this to be true.
In fact, our experience is so taken for granted that interactional
phenomena are often unrecognized.

Systems theory is a way of looking at interaction that makes
it available for therapy. Instead of dealing only with John the
alcoholic, we can attack the components of the way John and
Mary relate that feed into John's drinking and change those interactions in a way that frees both John and Mary from alcoholic
behavior.

Systems theory also gives us a new way of looking at cause
and effect in human interaction. Our logical patterns and our
very language box us into looking at events in sequences. The
idea of causality is grafted onto these sequences: *post hoc, ergo propter
hoc*. We say that Mary nags John. In the field of alcoholism,

we see the alcoholic as the victim of the family: family stresses add to the alcoholic's anxiety, becoming part of the complex that makes him drink. Or we see the family as the alcoholic's victim: "Years of living with an alcoholic is almost sure to make any wife or child neurotic," advises "The Big Book" (*Alcoholics Anonymous,* 1955, p. 122). This focus hampers therapeutic interventions. It makes us concentrate on the alcoholic to help him become more coping or focus on helping the family cope with the stresses of living with an alcoholic.

The systems model has a wider focus. Every individual is seen as acting and reacting in a causal chain that stretches so far back that the idea of cause and effect loses its importance. John had a hard day at work, so he came home and bolted two martinis, and when Mary asked shrewishly if he felt better now, he snapped at her. She was hurt, and he felt guilty because he knew that he was reacting not so much to her nagging as to his hard day, the fact that he sensed he was on his way to another sodden evening, and the fact that he had promised her and himself yesterday that he would limit himself to one sherry before dinner. Of course, if she did not nag him, he would stop. Only maybe she had had a hard day too, and it does not help when a husband comes home and bolts two martinis.

As alcoholism develops over a period of years, the family environment may deteriorate into an excellent breeding ground for serious problems. This can happen even while the individual alcoholic is in therapy, if family problems are ignored and the normal development of the family and each of its members is affected.

Characteristics of families with alcoholic members are very similar to the characteristics of violent families. Isolation, frustration, mistrust, low tolerance, fast reactivity, and often problems with sexuality and expression of feelings tend to be common. In fact in many cases, alcoholic families are also violent families. As Black (1982) said, there are similarities in the dynamics of alcoholism and battering. Alcoholics deny and minimize their abusive behavior, as do batterers. Both have the tendency to blame others and to avoid accepting the responsibility for their behavior. Family members, especially children, experience "two different people," the nice, caring parent who after a few drinks becomes a monster for no special reason. Both rationalize and have very good excuses for their behaviors.

The behaviors of the alcoholic and the batterer make them feel guilty and remorseful; they try to regain control and make promises they cannot keep. In most cases, theirs is a cycle that is repeated unless treated.

We do not yet have the research to show whether violence is due to an individual's intoxication. In many cases, we do not know whether the violent individual is using alcohol to express violence or whether it is the alcohol that is causing the violence. We cannot predict whether the violence will stop when the drinking stops, though often this is the case.

Alcohol is a mood changer, and frequently it triggers violent behavior. The violence may be taken for granted as part of the behavior of an intoxicated person by a family unfamiliar with what is normal and what is abnormal.

During the last decade, the mental health profession has begun to acknowledge family violence and to pay more attention to it. We are beginning to amass more data. We have learned that in the alcoholic, violent family, the parental team (which may be composed of two parents, parent and lover, mother and aunt, and so on) is almost always in conflict. Abusive alcoholic parents are commonly described as seeking satisfaction of their own need for comfort and nurturing from the children. Sometimes they expect the child to fulfill their needs and to make up for the deprivations they suffered in their own childhood or, in other cases, to give them the intimacy and caring they do not get in their relationship with their spouses.

The power struggle between the alcoholic incapable of functioning and the spouse or significant others who feel overwhelmed creates an environment of intolerance, frustration, anger, and abuse. The children receive mixed messages. One parent disqualifies the other, and discipline becomes difficult. Talking is often avoided to avoid confrontation. Feelings are not revealed. Little nurturing occurs in this environment of silence.

Between spouses, intimacy and closeness are hampered. Sex becomes the only way to feel closeness, and often as the alcoholism develops and gains ground, sex while intoxicated becomes unpleasant, then painful, and when the husband is the alcoholic, finally impossible. In some families, the child becomes a parent's sexual partner, through coercion or because sex is the only way for the child to feel close to the parent. Situational factors put children in the role of sexual partners, as described by one child in an alcoholic family: "I thought, now is my big chance to hold the family together, to keep my father from having to go out to drink, to go out and hire prostitutes, to keep him from going out with the guys and stay up all night and play poker" (Justice and Justice, 1969).

When children reach adolescence, the silence persists, and great damage may be done even in families in which active incest has not occurred. The pain of alcoholic parents or their partners, spilling into the sexual arena, can influence adolescents' view of the male-female relationship. When adolescents begin dating, parents may see them as "only out for sex." Normal development of sexuality has been curtailed, and only fear and guilt prevail. Lisa, age fifteen, was one of two daughters of Rita, an alcoholic. When family therapy began, it was clear that Rita, herself suffering from sexual problems, among others, was having severe difficulties accepting her daughter's growth. She mistrusted Lisa and frequently made cutting remarks about what she was "doing." One evening as Lisa was leaving for a date, Rita called her a whore. When Lisa described this in a therapy session, she wept. "Do you know what it feels like to have your mother call you a whore?"

The mental health profession ignored such issues for years. Focusing on the individual alcoholic, we ignored their families and children. It is vital to prevent the continuation of such patterns of behavior by working with the family unit and not isolating the individual.

As we work more with these families, we will learn more about them. One thing is clear, however: the violence of alcoholism is not a matter of perpetrator and victim. Its phenomena are systemic, and as we begin to study these issues we are in danger of missing their systemic components in our anxiety to protect the victim (Flanzer, 1982). We must guard against being simplistic here.

Mark, an alcoholic, bought his wife, Maria, a beautiful pair of earrings as a Christmas present. Four nights before Christmas, he got drunk and slapped her. The next morning he gave her the earrings. She threw them at him. Mark exploded. Feeling rejected, he pulled out of the closet all the presents they had bought for the children and destroyed them one by one. When Maria tried to stop him, he slapped her to the floor and kicked her, breaking two of her ribs. When Maria discussed the incident with a therapist, she was contrite. "I know I shouldn't have thrown those earrings at him," she said. "I know it was my fault."

It is not "blaming the victim" to ask why so many victims of alcoholic violence react in precisely this fashion. It delineates an area that we must explore.

To move beyond a focus on the individual alcoholic to a broader focus seems to be only common sense. It is an effort that must always be incomplete, but it is a step toward taking into account more of the components of the syndrome. Its effect on therapy is to open whole new fields for possible therapeutic intervention.

Self-help groups like AA and Rational Recovery (RR) become more than ever a strong network of support, more so since many other groups are available to help the individual deal with issues related to addiction, as well as to other destructive behaviors, such as gambling, sex, and so on.

We still have all the ways of helping John, the individual alcoholic: psychotherapy, behavioral therapy, and medical care. In addiction to the focus on the individual, the systems model gives us a way of looking at the context of the alcoholic syndrome and intervening to change it. The alcoholic is neither victim nor victimizer. His behavior and the way he thinks and feels are the result of a whole chain of human interactions. Individual methods of helping the alcoholic have to work with only one link. With the systems model, many other approaches to change become possible.

2

~~~~~~~~~~~

Family Therapy
and Alcoholic Families

Definitions of "the family" fill volumes in anthropology, sociology, and psychology. In therapeutic terms, however, a family can be defined rather simply. It is a group of people with a history of life in common. The composition of a family is not the significant factor. A family may be a mother and daughter; or a household composed of two parents, their children, their children's spouses, and the grandchildren; or two lesbians living together with their children; or it may be the "average American" nuclear family. What is significant is that these groups of people have evolved ways of living together and that these ways of living form a structure that governs the way these people behave and feel.

The easiest way to explore and describe the family in therapeutic terms is to present a paradigm. So let us postulate, following the family therapist Salvador Minuchin (1974), that a family begins when two people join with the purpose of forming a family. This paradigm, as Minuchin points out, is a construct that has as much validity for any individual family as does the "average American family with its 2.2 children." But unlike the average American family, this model gives us a framework for looking at any individual client family against the background of some sort of norm.

Couple Formation: A Paradigm

Let us say that a man and a woman, whom we will call Art and Nancy, have decided to get married. These two individuals have decided to become a couple. A new social group has been delineated. As Thomas Hardy puts it in *Jude the Obscure:* "And so, standing before the aforesaid officiator, the two swore that at every other time of their lives till death took them, they would assuredly believe, feel, and desire precisely as they had believed, felt, and desired during the few preceding weeks."

The decision to marry (or move in together) is a milestone for Art and Nancy, as for any other couple. But their relationship does not spring into being with this decision. Forming a viable dyadic unit is still very much in process. Art and Nancy have been "seeing each other" for six months now. Deeply in love, they are delighted with the process of learning about each other. Art has discovered that Nancy cannot balance her checkbook. He does not see this as a problem; in fact, secretly he considers it adorably feminine. He will, of course, manage their combined incomes. Nancy too assumes that Art will handle financial matters; she sees no difficulty with his suggestion that they pool their accounts.

Marriage does not only mean living together. It involves growing up together, developing a relationship that will be a source of strength not only in its own little world but in the outside world. It is a building of intimacy in an environment of nurturance and trust (Calderone, 1983).

Art and Nancy have already begun to learn to tune into each other's feelings and moods. Now this knowledge is expanding. Art knows that Nancy's department at work is horrible on Wednesdays because of the weekly closing. If she snaps at him on Wednesday evening, he teases her about "closingitis." Soon it is accepted between them that Wednesday is a day in which Nancy does not want to have to think about anything but her job.

Art has his moments too. He never loses his temper, but Nancy is learning to listen for a certain edge to his voice, and without realizing it, she tends to leave him alone until the edge disappears.

In the terminology of family therapy, Art and Nancy are developing the transactional patterns that form the structure of the spouse subsystem. These patterns, often developed with no conscious effort or recognition, operate in ways that become automatic. It is accepted between them that Art is the wit. If Nancy ventures to tell a joke at a party, Art will be slightly startled. His quickly concealed surprise will make Nancy wonder uneasily whether she is stealing his thunder, and next time it will be Art who tells the joke.

Some transactional patterns are the result of specific open negotiation, and they are policed by the couple after being attained by discussion and compromise. Both Art and Nancy hate to shop in crowded stores, but Saturday morning is the only time they have. Therefore Nancy will do the shopping, but Art will drive the car down and pick her up. This is only fair. Other patterns, not specifically negotiated, cannot be rationally agreed on. Art and Nancy both think that husband and wife should share the household drudgery. But Nancy's father, not otherwise a househusband, always took the garbage out. Therefore Nancy assumes that Art's jobs include emptying the garbage. If he "forgets," she finds herself weeping in a fury of genuine betrayal, to the bewilderment of them both. The issue has become more than the chore. The issue is also Nancy's sense of self and her expectations of herself and of Art. Art's and Nancy's conscious and unconscious expectations will have to be worked through and somehow resolved during the long process, which is never entirely finished, of forming a marriage.

One of the couple is an alcoholic in a very early stage. Let us assume it is Art, although it could just as easily be Nancy. Neither Art nor Nancy recognizes Art's drinking as a problem. He gets a little high now and then—who doesn't? Last week, he got so drunk at a party that Nancy insisted on driving home, but he had had an awfully hard day. Nancy's mother jokes that the way to handle a man is to stand at the apartment door with a gin and a glass. "As long as it takes him to walk from the elevator to the door, that's how long you pour." Art just loves a good time. And he wants a wife who will join him in a life of love and companionship. They will have fun—enjoy parties and their friends.

When alcoholism appears early in a relationship, denial may also appear from the start. This is very characteristic of families affected by alcoholism. Incipient alcoholics and their spouses are rarely equipped to face the problem. Instead they try to ignore it. Nancy's tactful "I'll drive, dear," is becoming more and more of a habit. But it is a habit they can live with.

If drinking worsens, however, the necessity of dealing with the problem without acknowledging it complicates unresolved tensions in the relationship. One Saturday morning, Nancy shakes Art awake and tells him she is going shopping; he should meet her in an hour. Three hours later, she finally takes a cab home to find that Art, having tried the hair of the dog for his hangover, is still sleeping it off. Nancy puts all the groceries away by herself and does not speak to Art for the rest of the afternoon. By evening, things are back to normal, though Art secretly resolves he will not do that again, and Nancy silently promises herself that next Saturday she will make Art drive her down and wait.

As time goes on, drinking influences more and more of the couple's activities. Nancy finds excuses to stay away from family gatherings because Art got so drunk at Thanksgiving. For the same reason, she stops planning the dinner parties they both enjoyed. As his life begins to center more and more on drinking, so does hers. Nancy does the shopping alone now. She also balances the checkbook and in fact handles most of the chores. Formerly a meticulous housekeeper, she begins to let things slide. The trash piles up because that is still Art's job, but that is not the only messy spot in their lives. Art, once also a meticulous housekeeper, hates the way the apartment looks as much as she does, but he is in no position to launch a protest that might start a discussion of what is going on with them.

By now, the couple's transactional patterns are organized around the fact that Art's functioning is impaired much of the time. Communications between the spouses have become sparse and ridden with guilt and anger. Negotiating and resolving conflict are hampered because confrontation is contrary to the patterns they have developed or "everything would be all right if Art didn't drink so much." In a surprising number of families, however, the problem is never stated that specifically. Many "Arts" and "Nancys" go for years without acknowledging what is happening. A problem that is acknowledged must be dealt with in some way. If Nancy confronted Art with his drinking, he might leave her or she might have to leave him. In any case, she would have to do something, and she has no idea of what to do. She is very angry, and he is very guilty, but there is no way out.

If alcoholism appeared in one spouse's family of origin, that can profoundly affect the formation of the spouse unit. Patterns of the family of origin are perpetuated in every couple's relationship. These patterns may interfere with the capacity of the couple to achieve a healthy relationship. Giving, trusting, and intimacy are experiences learned from parents. Some parents do not have the background to draw on to provide a good model for their children.

A woman whose father is an alcoholic will probably bring to the marriage the idea that a man cannot manage authority. This becomes part of her expectations of the marital unit. She may hate her father's alcoholism and desire nothing more than to make a new and different life for herself. But she expects men to be relatively passive. Unless this problem can be worked through, a skew in the roles of husband and wife, which will affect the family throughout its existence, may develop.

Nancy does not know that her father is an alcoholic. He was never available to her — she can remember long conversations with her mother and very little contact with him. It does not occur to her that her mother taught her that the man is the head of the family, while showing her that a man cannot handle that job without the behind-the-scenes management of a loyal wife. Nancy only knows that it seems natural to her to take over the jobs that Art is not performing, though she resents the drain on her time and energy.

Art, guilty and confused about his own drinking, experiences himself as disqualified by his wife. But it is not his way to confront matters. If he faced the problems that exist, he might have to control his drinking or admit that he cannot. In any case, he would have to do something, and he has no idea of what to do.

As everything else in their relationship deteriorates, so does the couple's enjoyment of sex. Nancy has begun to join

Art in an evening drink. Sometimes they go out for a walk, which ends in the bar around which Art's social life is more and more centered. When they get home, Nancy goes to bed. Art sits down with a nightcap to watch TV. Eventually he gropes his way to bed and falls asleep. Sometimes he falls asleep in his chair. Nancy does not make an issue of it — that is not her way. And in a sense, this is a good arrangement for her. Nancy has never truly enjoyed intercourse, and now, with the resentments of the years building up, she would just as soon not sleep with Art. The fact that Art is drinking himself into a stupor most nights takes away from her responsibility for looking at her own sexual desires; his drinking takes her off the hook.

Nancy throws herself into her work, or has an affair, or in many cases begins abusing alcohol herself. Or she goes to a doctor, crying that she is exhausted, that she cannot handle everything, that Art drinks too much. The doctor writes a prescription for tranquilizers, and now both spouses float through the evening. In any case, the potential for love, support, and growth within this marriage seems to have evaporated.

For the purposes of illustration, let us now take Art and Nancy to the next step of the family paradigm. Nancy gets pregnant (if Nancy is an alcoholic, fetal damage is a real possibility). They begin to plan for the child.

As mentioned earlier, we all bring into the family life patterns of our own family of origin. Regardless of these patterns, the new family requires family members to learn to live together, especially when children are involved. Additional functions are added — to teach how to give, to receive love, and to support each other in mutual development and fulfillment.

The child is not real to Art yet, though he swears that he is going to be a good father. His children will have everything he never had. Nancy is planning to switch to part-time work. She will have a baby and her job — a full life — and do it all magnificently. A nagging unease about Art is pushed aside. Fatherhood will make a new man out of him.

The birth of a baby, however desired and planned for, presents new and urgent problems to any couple. In family therapy terms, the transactional patterns must be modified. The spouse subsystem still exists, but now there are also a parental subsystem, a mother-child subsystem, a father-child subsystem, new relationships to the grandparents and extended family, baby-sitters, the pediatrician, and the other mothers in the park who monitor the infant's development with all the benevolence of Harpies. Or so it seems to Nancy. Nancy feels that she gets scant attention these days. Within a few days, she has gone from "Sit down, honey," to "Nan, the baby's crying!" Art, too, feels aggrieved and neglected. Nancy's only working part-time now, so for Pete's sake, why isn't dinner ready? She has not even mixed the martinis, so he mixes the pitcher himself and pours a little heavily. Later, when Janie is finally asleep, Nancy turns to Art. "I'm going to bed," he mumbles. "Hard day."

In families affected by alcoholism, the drinking problem may not have been too much of a strain on spouse transactions. When a family consists only of two adults, an unstructured life is easy to deal with. You do not get up on Saturday because you have a hangover. Both of you sleep until noon, and chores can wait. The birth of a child causes a radical change. Someone must be sober enough to feed the infant and to supervise the toddler. In time, supper will have to be served early enough to allow the grade-schooler to do her homework.

If alcoholism is in the family, typically it will have been growing worse during the years of marriage. During the early childhood years it begins to make a real impact on the family unit. Now the family must be kept going. And it is the nonalcoholic spouse who has to do it. Sometimes the nonalcoholic spouse collapses into depression, alcoholism, or illness. But in a surprising number of cases, the nonalcoholic spouse pulls himself together and keeps things going, at least after a fashion. This can go on for years.

In many cases the alcoholic is a wife and mother who does not work outside the home. Her alcoholism is relatively easy to conceal. Someone who works outside the home has to be on the job, more or less on time, and more or less functional. Progressing alcoholism tends to be picked up relatively early by the supervisor or co-worker or the alcoholic herself, who realizes she is not measuring up in the vitally important area of the world of work. A housewife can conceal drinking more success-fully. This picture is changing as more and more women join the work force. But the problem of the "alcoholic housewife" re-mains very much part of the picture of alcoholism.

Today an increasing number of women are reaching out for treatment (Beckman and Amaro, 1984), especially young women. This increase is also being seen in the affiliations to AA (34 percent are women). But the stigma of being diagnosed as an alcoholic, and in particular the myth that women alco-holics are promiscuous, keep many women from reaching out for help.

In our paradigm family, however, the alcoholic is Art. So it is Nancy who takes over. She fathers and mothers the chil-dren and takes on as many of the other family tasks as she can, including keeping up a good front. Art cannot possibly work with Little League; he is far too tired on weekends. But she will be glad to chair the fund-raising committee.

Studies of wives of alcoholics have characterized them as power-driven women who knowingly or subconsciously married an alcoholic because he was a man they could dominate. But this is a view that results from focusing on the problem from the point of view of the individual. When we focus on the alco-holic individual, we see his wife as an adjunct/contributor to the picture. When we look at them as a couple, we see the non-alcoholic partner taking on increased executive functioning to compensate for the alcoholic's incapacity. This behavior unques-tionably feeds back into the alcoholic's difficulties. It is also true that the alcoholic's difficulties force the nonalcoholic partner to supersede him.

The result in family terms is as unfortunate as the results in individual terms. The alcoholic is pushed to the periphery of the family, while the better-functioning family members get on with the business of life. Often he excludes himself, out of guilt. This behavior helps cement an alliance of spouse and chil-dren, who blame the alcoholic member for the family unhappi-ness. Transactional patterns based on compensating for his dis-ability develop. Eventually any attempt on his part to reenter will become a threat to the family's structure.

In many families, the children grow up in a conspiracy of silence. Daddy is the head of the family; everyone agrees on that. Mommy does the shopping, the cooking, the bill paying, and in fact most things that get done. Daddy does not, so the children learn to help. Daddy is "too tired." And he had "a hard day at work." Again, Hardy, in *Tess of the D'Urbervillles,* presents a telling vignette: "'The poor man can't go . . .' Tess sat up in bed . . . 'But somebody must go,' she replied. 'It is late for the hives already . . .' Mrs. Durbeyfield looked unequal to the emergency. 'Some young-feller, perhaps would go? One of them who were so much after dancing with 'ee yesterday,' she presently suggested. 'Oh no — I wouldn't have it for the world!' declared Tess proudly. 'And letting everybody know the reason — such a thing to be ashamed of! I think I could go.'"

In families affected by alcoholism, the older children typically take on parental and executive functions rather early. A first grader comes home afternoon after afternoon to find her mother "napping" heavily on the couch. She takes her little brother out of the playpen and minds him until her father comes home. Then she helps him start dinner. A boy who finds that his Saturday boat rides with his father get as far as the boathouse bar eventually elects to stay home, where he helps his mother with the household chores. The children's maturity helps stabilize the family, but often this is a pseudomaturity, inappropriately assumed at the expense of childhood developmental tasks.

Children may even become involved in transactions that ought to be bounded within the spouse subsystem. They group around the nonalcoholic parent, and while the older son takes on many of the parenting tasks, the oldest daughter becomes the housewife. Middle children typically escape from the family as soon as possible. But smaller children may have to remain the babies of the family, even when they are well into their teens. The parent stays close to them, "taking good care of the children" but also finding a closeness he or she needs in this relationship.

In family therapy terms, the family has developed a workable structure that compensates for the inadequacy of a vital family member. But both spouses lack the support of a spouse subsystem. The children lack the nurturance and protection of effective parenting. Everybody lacks the support that would make it possible to experiment and grow.

Janie is fourteen now, but she does not date; she has to get dinner and do the dishes. Her brother, Tom, does not want to join Little League. Even children whose parents are divorced bring their fathers to the game. But he cannot ask Art to come or to pitch while he practices batting.

The family is organized around its problem member. Nancy and the children tacitly blame Art's drinking for all problems, and they long for his recovery, but a cure would actually be a threat to the family structure. A sober Art would have to be allowed to act as husband and father, and such a change would put the whole family into unexplored territory.

The next developmental stage of the paradigm family is reached when the children approach adulthood. Now the children are or should be moving out on their own. The children were the ones who kept the spouses together. (Nancy has been telling herself for years that she stayed with Art "for the children's sake.") Now the two spouses are alone again, and they must again develop a dyadic relationship. At the same time, they must cope with basic changes in their own lives: the loss of parents, the sense that one's own time is running out, and perhaps a perceived loss of sexual attractiveness. Many drinking problems develop or intensify at this stage.

In our paradigm family, Art's drinking has worsened over the years. "Occasional relief drinking" has turned to constant and perhaps surreptitious drinking. He experiences memory blackouts and other symptoms of disability that he cannot ignore. But at the same time that recognition of the problem can no longer be denied, his dependency on alcohol increases. By now he is addicted physiologically as well as psychologically, and persistent remorse and guilt are combined with grandiose and aggressive behavior. Eventually physical deterioration will contribute to the onset of lengthy intoxications.

For all these years, Nancy has stood by Art with a Griselda-like loyalty that is both admirable and destructive. She has called the office to say he was sick whenever he was too hung over to make it in. She has stopped seeing family and friends, partly because it is so much of an effort to keep up appearances and partly because she never knows what shape Art will be in. She has remained loving, protective, and concerned. Yet her loving acts have fed into the problem, reinforcing Art's incapacity and probably adding to a growing load of resentment and guilt on his part; distress and martyrdom on hers.

The extended family and friends have caught on. The word has sped around the family network, and Art is firmly identified as "a problem." Nancy has confided in a few close friends, and their sympathy buttresses her self-image as the noble martyr. They relate to Art with a sympathy that clearly conveys that he is not quite on an equal footing. Again the problem is not acknowledged, for as long as Art and Nancy do not confront it, it would be very difficult for anyone else in the family to do so. Besides, what could they do?

In the world of work, Art's colleagues react with an anxious patience. Alcoholics frequently experience their friends as "acting funny." This is not a paranoid ideation: it is an accurate perception of the friends' attempts to help with the problem without dealing with it directly. The boss, with the best of intentions, takes Art off a challenging assignment and puts him in conditions that will be less stressful for the poor guy. The next morning, Art is sick as a pup. His supervisor and closest friend do the estimate he was supposed to work on, give it to him to sign, and then send him home to "rest." The bowling team also rallies around. It becomes a regular thing for someone to drive Art home. These are concerned and adaptive responses, but they deprive the alcoholic of validation as a mature, responsible person.

The story of this paradigm can have many endings. In some cases, Art goes to AA or RR meetings. Rational Recovery is based on the philosophy of rational emotive therapy. Individuals are expected to acknowledge their own helplessness against drinking instead of considering themselves sick. As described in *The Small Book,* this alternative group to AA emphasizes the personal responsibility of the individual, and as a consequence, the individual alcoholic is responsible for kicking the habit instead of leaning on a higher power (Trimpey, 1989). For some alcoholics like Art, the appeal to forces within oneself simply works better. Each individual has to choose the group that fits best with his or her own needs.

In a less happy scenario, Art's drinking problems continue. When the younger child enters college, Nancy divorces Art and moves to another city. Or Art leaves the family and drops out of sight. Nancy rears the children, all of them saddened, but also more than a little relieved to have him gone.

In some cases, even though Art may eventually recover from alcoholism, he and Nancy have grown so far apart by now that this makes little difference to their relationship. But they stay together; where else would Nancy go? By now she is comfortable with the absence of challenge and growth, and she would have no idea of what to do with her life.

For the purposes of this book, however, something brings our paradigm family to the attention of the mental health field. How does a therapist approach a problem like Art and Nancy's? The first step is to identify alcoholism as the major problem and to deal with it if necessary.

Often alcoholism is not what brings the family affected by alcoholism to therapy. The patterns of denial still exist. It is not uncommon for members of the helping profession to treat an alcoholic family and never to be told about the drinking problem. Truancy, acting out in school, severe depression — many presenting problems may actually relate back to an alcoholism that the family is still denying or concealing.

In general, therapy has two main goals. One is to open the drinking problem to discussion and to therapy if possible. The alcoholism must be dealt with. The second is to change the patterns that are keeping these people entrapped in the network of alcoholic-and-participants. If at all possible, the individual should be helped to attain sobriety. But this is only the first step. The sobered alcoholic is still living in social systems organized around his incapacity. For everyone closely involved with an alcoholic, sobriety is a radical change. It may be something each has longed for. But it is a change that will require them to do and see things differently. Nancy, for instance, has gained weight over the years and has let her appearance go. Now she can no longer blame her unhappiness on Art's drinking. She is a potentially attractive woman in her late forties, but she has lost sight of any possibilities other than mother/ grandmother and wife of an alcoholic Now that Art is no longer drinking, what is she to do?

Whenever possible, therapy should focus on the family, changing the patterns that have grown up around the alcoholism, that are fed by it and feeding into it. Individual therapy often takes these patterns into account in a nonconstructive way by defining the spouse and family as part of the enemy that the alcoholic has to fight to stay sober. Self-help groups, too, may fail to help the individual learn to act more effectively in the groups in which he lives. It is not at all uncommon for an alcoholic to work intensively with AA, for his partner to work with Al-Anon, and for both of them to reach a stage where their new individual gains are incompatible with their relationship. A therapy that focuses on changing the family into a network that supports the alcoholic as a sober, functioning member and that continues to act as a source of support and growth for all family members is obviously the better strategy.

Therapeutic Implications of the Family Systems Model

This book is not a textbook of family therapy. Its purpose is rather to present cases in which the principles and techniques of family therapy were used to help alcoholic families. Some of the many excellent presentations of theory and technique are listed in the References (Minuchin, 1974, 1981; Haley, 1968, 1976).

Very briefly, however, family therapy conceptualizes the family as a human social system — a group of humans who develop, in the course of their lives in common, a superstructure that affects the way they behave toward each other and to the world at large.

The family system is organized into subsystems — individuals, generational groups, and groups delineated by gender, function, common interest, or simply mutual liking. These units are constantly affecting each other, and any change in one unit will affect all the others to a greater or lesser degree.

The family system exists within other systems made up of the extended family, the community, the region, the country, and the immediate world. Society demands certain tasks from the family, and changes in society require changes in the family. At the same time, the family must maintain continuity; it has the main responsibility for giving individuals a sense of belonging—a sense of where they "come from."

The interphases of all subsystems, from the individual/individual up to the nation/world, are called *boundaries*. The function of a boundary is to delineate the group, while giving it access to information from other groups. A boundary must separate and protect; it must also unite and give access. Much of the work of family therapy focuses on these boundaries within the family, exploring and modifying the way a husband (an individual subsystem) relates to his wife, the way the spouse subsystem relates to the sibling subsystem, and so on.

An individual is a subsystem of the family as well as a person in her own right. If our focus is an individual alcoholic and we change her, we will also change her family, intentionally or not. In family therapy, the focus will be changing the network of family relationship forces rather than the alcoholic member alone. In many cases the therapeutic target will be a dyad, a triad, or the interactions of a larger relationship.

Therapy with families affected by alcoholism has two major foci. One is combatting the problems posed by alcoholism. The other is helping this individual family attain their best possible functioning. This help requires knowledge beyond expertise in alcoholism and family functioning.

For many years, therapists working in the field of alcoholism ignored some symptoms that could be related to psychiatric problems. Some thought they would take care of psychiatric problems in treating the alcoholism. Because of the evolution of treatment, we are beginning to understand that some of the symptoms may help establish a primary and secondary diagnosis. The alcoholic may display symptoms of other psychiatric disorders that can be the consequence of heavy drinking or of a preexisting disorder. Only after the drinking stops can a clear diagnosis be established. The individual can then be treated as an alcoholic patient or as an alcoholic patient with a psychiatric disorder. Both fields must be aware of the problems of treating only one syndrome (Mulinski, 1989; Helzer and others, 1988; Schuckit, 1983).

The therapist must also take into account the family's ethnic background. Strengthening the boundaries around the nuclear family is probably an incorrect approach to the problems of an Italian-American family whose grandmother is accepted as the matriarch. The family's developmental stages should also be considered in the therapeutic approach. The goal may be to help a sobered father learn to take on parental functions. If he is dealing with a young child, the emphasis will be on nurturance and guidance. If he is dealing with an adolescent, the therapist will have to help the father learn to negotiate, maintaining the authority of a parent while remaining flexible enough to allow the adolescent to grow and separate.

The variety of family types includes the intact nuclear family with parents and children living together, remarried couples with stepchildren, couples without children, families with adult children living away but still involved in family affairs, multigenerational families, single-parent families, nonmarried heterosexual or homosexual couples living together, engaged or involved couples living separately, and long-term roommates not sexually involved. Given this range, a therapist has to be open-minded and avoid labeling before making an assessment of the needs of the family she will be treating.

The family paradigm gives the therapist not only a way of looking at a client family but also a direction for therapy. It can also help separate the significant from the unimportant. A therapist might have problems working with a family whose parents beat the children as a method of discipline. But because the therapeutic goal is to help the parents assert their parental authority, the therapist can focus correctly on rewarding this parental assertion rather than attacking the method used. These general principles will be illustrated again and again in the case examples that follow. Therefore let us take the plunge and consider how therapy can be initiated with an alcoholic or with a family affected by alcoholism.

The first family interview is a time for the therapist to assess each member's position in the family. Having attained a working diagnosis of the family's structure, she will then start working to move each family member in a way that begins correcting the structural skews caused by alcoholism.

The problem of alcoholism itself will have to be acknowledged and sometimes dealt with. In some families, this is easy; alcoholism is the presenting problem. Giuseppi mentioned his drinking when he called to make the appointment for the first interview. He said he had been a heavy drinker for almost twenty years, before stopping a year and a half ago. Now he was drinking again, and he felt himself slipping into old patterns. A family interview was arranged in which Giuseppi's drinking was the first order of business.

Ian sought therapy for marital problems. He said he wanted to explore his relationship with his wife, to keep the family together. In the first session he talked almost exclusively about his relationship with his wife. She was neglecting herself and had stopped trying to attract him sexually. He had entered some extramarital relationships as a method of seeking sexual gratification.

Only when he was saying good-bye did he casually mention, "By the way, I probably should tell you that I think I have a drinking problem." The therapist shared with him that she had picked that up during the session. His eyes were very red, his face was swollen, and although he was not a heavy man, he had a large stomach. The therapist told him that she thought they would have to talk about this and made an appointment for the next day to focus on Ian's drinking. Alcoholism was affecting his work and his relationship with his children, to say nothing of his marriage. Unquestionably it was a serious problem, affecting not only the spouse but also the whole family.

Riva also presented her problem as a marital conflict. While the therapist was talking with her, it became clear that these marital problems were related to her husband's drinking.

Through her seeking therapy, her husband and daughter were brought into treatment that dealt with her husband's drinking as well as what it had done to the family.

In other cases, even alcoholism of long duration is deliberately concealed. Mary, a twenty-year-old divorcée and mother of a two-year-old daughter, came to therapy after hospitalization for severe depression. She had been abusing drugs for years but was not using them when she entered the psychiatric ward. After admission, she became completely withdrawn. A family session was arranged with the participation of Mary, her baby, and her parents, with whom Mary was again living. As the session progressed and it became apparent that Mary insisted on remaining mute, the therapist decided to split the family group by sending the father out to an adjacent room where he could observe his wife and daughter through a one-way mirror.

The therapist's purpose was to see whether the mother and daughter could open up in the father's absence. But when the cotherapist sat beside Mr. McCarthy behind the mirror, she was struck by the strong smell of alcohol on his breath though it was only 9:15 A.M. She asked Mr. McCarthy to rejoin his family and immediately confronted him, "Were you drinking before the session?"

Now that the problem was out in the open, Mary suddenly began to talk. She spoke of her own experiences with alcohol and her strong resentment toward her father for having used her as a drinking partner while she was in her early teens. At this point, the focus changed from a depressed, uncooperative young adult to the alcoholism in the family which had been covered up by all the family members for years.

In the Giacomelli family, the mother, Anina, was an alcoholic. The entire family concealed the problem. The family came into therapy after the father called a mental health center to request help for Anina. But he reported only that she was suffering from severe depression.

Anina herself believed that no one knew of her drinking. She disguised her frequent periods of incapacity as headaches, and everyone in the family, extended family, neighborhood, and church politely maintained this fiction. In the first family session, however, the therapist picked up some clues that Anina might have a drinking problem. Only in her thirties, Anina looked like a woman in her fifties. She was overweight, her eyes were red, and her face was suspiciously puffy. The therapist began to explore with the family what Anina's life was like. The youngest child, Julian, age six, let the cat out of the bag, and within minutes the entire family was sharing their feelings about Anina's drinking. Shocked by the realization that everyone not only knew of her drinking but hated it, Anina attempted suicide. She had to be rushed to the emergency room. But therapy, which began again as soon as possible, could now focus both on the drinking and on the family problems it created.

Whether alcoholism is acknowledged or uncovered during the course of therapy, the family therapist must establish a therapeutic contract with the entire family plus the alcoholic member. It must be understood that therapy will deal with the drinking problem *and* with the problems of the entire family. Ideally work on sobriety can be done while family problems are attacked in a mutually reinforcing multimodal strategy.

It is often desirable to hold individual sessions with the alcoholic concurrently with early family sessions. In these individual sessions, the therapist can get a good history to determine the stage of the alcoholism. Medical referrals may be desirable. Ego strength in the alcoholic can be built up, and any accomplishment can be praised and reinforced to increase self-esteem. Close, perhaps daily, contact may be necessary. The therapist may set a time for daily phone contact, which maintains communication, supports the alcoholic, and also begins the process of helping the alcoholic establish a routine for his or her life.

AA can be very useful here. The contact with people who have experienced what he is experiencing is invaluable to the patient, as is the support of the group. Furthermore, AA can be continually available as a therapist cannot be, and its members know how to deal with those crisis situations that the patient has not yet learned to cope with.

Individual sessions with the alcoholic plus his participation in AA make it possible to de-emphasize the drinking problem in the family sessions. Teaching the family about alcoholism is often an important step. They must learn that alcoholism is an illness and to adjust to it as they would to any other chronic illness in a family member. But they must also learn not to blame alcoholism for all problems that arise. The therapist must point out that the individual alcoholic is working on his or her drinking. Individual work will be done with other family members if necessary, or they may be referred to Al-Anon or Alateen (Ablon, 1974).

In the process, the therapist will work with the spouses on the spouse relationship (Bepko and others, 1985; Berenson, 1976). Some sessions with them will center on their roles as parents. Sessions with the children will help them turn over the parental and executive roles they have inappropriately assumed and will help them find compensations for this change in age-appropriate ways.

Children of alcoholic families have been ignored in the recovery process for years. The patterns of behavior learned at home were repeated, and a new generation of alcoholics developed. We must stop the continuation of this pattern. It is not all right to start drinking because the father drinks or the mother drinks. We have to help this generation of potential alcoholics take the responsibility for their behavior, build up their self-esteem, and not feel helpless, guilty, or responsible for their parents' drinking. Literature is available today to tackle this serious subject as soon as we start to work with the family.

The interventions chosen will depend on the individual family and therapist. But the goal of therapy is a better-functioning family unit.

Today many rehabilitation programs offer services for the family as well as for the individual. Most of these services begin with educational lectures about alcoholism. In the process of learning about the problems created by the alcoholism of the individual member, the other members learn to take responsibility for their own lives and to stop scapegoating the alcoholic.

Al-Anon teaches its members to "detach," but the significance of the detachment is often misunderstood. I believe that detachment can well be conceptualized with the idea of "codependency." According to Potter-Efron and Potter-Efron (1989), "a codependent is an individual who has been significantly affected in specific ways by current or past involvements in an alcoholic, chemically dependent, or other long-term stressful family environment."

We find in the literature a set of characteristics given to these individuals that in many ways are similar to those of some adult children of alcoholics. Let us use the labels, but let us teach all these individuals not only to understand their behaviors but also to learn new ones. Family members are "shaped" and "constrained" by the behavior of all the other members and individuals and as a group. Family therapy becomes the most advisable method to deal with alcoholism.

The family life organizes around the alcoholism of one of its members, and it is regulated by its development (Steinglass and others, 1987). As a consequence, the life of the family accommodates according to its demands. Individuals have to learn to manage day-to-day life and to deal not only with crisis situations.

~~~~~~~~~

Part 2

Alcoholic Families
in Therapy

3

~~~~~~~~~~

Rebuilding
Family Patterns:
The Williamses

Helping the alcoholic attain sobriety is not enough. This is shown by the many cases in which families continue growth-hampering family patterns even though drinking behavior has disappeared.

In the Williams family, both parents were alcoholics with a twenty-year history of problem drinking. The spouses had separated for four years, during which they had worked individually on their drinking problems through AA and treatment with different individual therapists. Finally they had reconciled for the sake of their children. At this point, Paul had been sober for a year and a half, and Janet for eight months, but sobriety was not enough. The couple felt unable to integrate their individual growth into their relationship as husband and wife, and this difficulty was hampering their individual work. Janet felt she needed a man in the house to be her co-parent, but she did not want to relate to Paul sexually or to fulfill his other demands as a husband in a relationship that did not include drinking. She simply did not know Paul as a sober man. But both Janet and Paul were willing to work at becoming better parents. Consequently a family session was arranged. At this stage, they both felt much more comfortable working as parents than as spouses.

Whatever the individual problem or presenting problem may be, the entire family becomes the patient. In the first session, therefore, both parents and children were present and the therapist began to assess the family's existing structure. The younger children, Jean, age thirteen, and Bob, age eleven, complained in the session that their brother Fred, age eighteen, bossed them around. The therapist inferred that Fred had become the substitute father for the younger children. Thus one treatment goal was immediately obvious: to help Fred step down from his role as substitute father, while helping Paul reestablish himself as the father. This was not conveyed to the family, but the therapist mentally formulated three steps toward that goal. The family would have to (1) recognize the existing family structure, which included Fred's dysfunctional displacement of his father, (2) see that displacement as undesirable, and (3) understand that this confusion of roles was the result of a long period of parental drinking but that the parents were now capable of acting as parents.

The therapist raised the subject of alcoholism and how it had affected the family. Everyone denied that this had ever been a problem. Fred, who often acted as family spokesperson, said, "You have the wrong idea. There was never any lack of food in the house." The therapist persisted, asking who took care of the household chores, such as cleaning. Paul Jr., fifteen, grimaced and pointed to himself. This was another example of a child's stepping into an executive role as a direct consequence of the behavior of alcoholic parents. While drinking, they had in effect become absent members of the family.

As the session continued, the position of each member of the family became clearer. Fred was a parental child whose authoritarian behavior had been supported by his mother. Paul Jr., who had assumed some of his mother's tasks in doing the household chores, was referred to by her as the good boy of the family. The two youngest children were withdrawn but seemed much younger than their ages. Jean, at age thirteen, had closed off communication with her family in order to avoid their overwhelming expectations. Her older sister had taken care of the whole family before marrying at the age of seventeen, perhaps as a way of opting out of the family conflicts. Everyone compared Jean with that sister, urging her to be neater and more diligent. Bob, at age eleven, used baby talk. Throughout the session, the mother corrected the children's behavior, telling them to speak up or to sit straight, remarking, "You should have washed your hands before we got here," or "tied your shoes," and so on. It seemed obvious that Janet babied the children, probably so that she could keep herself busy in the role of a mother with young children who needed constant attention.

The father was an outsider, only now beginning to relate to his family but doing so mostly as a disciplinarian. His attempts to be a good father were sincere, but his contact with his children tended to be confined to lecturing.

The first session was largely exploratory. But at its end, Paul Sr. pointed out that this was the first time in years the family had been able "to sit together and talk without yelling and screaming." The family left the session with a feeling of hope. Lines of communication had been reopened. The two parental children were beginning to realize that their parental functioning was inappropriate, and the parents were recognizing that their drinking had pushed the children into roles from which they now needed to be freed.

The therapeutic goal with the Williams family was to change the interactions that kept the children in executive positions and the parents as incompetents. In particular, Paul Jr. and Fred would have to return executive authority to their parents and to find developmentally appropriate compensations for this ceding of power.

To accomplish this, Paul and Janet would have to learn to support each other as parents. One approach to this problem was spouse sessions in which the therapist encouraged the couple to work on their relationship. Part of the problem was Paul's long and irregular working hours. Supported by the therapist and by Janet's statement that she needed him at home, Paul was able to confront his boss and tell him he would no longer be available for unlimited overtime. Fortunately Paul had already reached a point in his recovery where he did not have to compensate by proving to himself that he was a good provider.

As Paul began to spend more time with his family, he was able to practice supportive ways of acting as a husband and father. Naturally this change did not come easily. The homeostatic mechanisms that keep a family functioning in its usual manner have great power. For example, when Janet and

Paul were drinking, the family had had no regular mealtimes. One of the things the couple wanted to establish as a ritual symbolizing their new life was a regular dinner hour. But almost every night, one of the children was late. Still, the improvement in the spouse relationship was supporting change. Janet was learning to express anger openly instead of covertly punishing Paul by rejecting him sexually. Gradually the couple were working their way toward mutual support as they resumed their roles as parents.

Bob, the youngest son, was the first to react visibly to this family change. He had been very close to his mother, often even sleeping in her bed. When his father came home, he felt displaced. To him, the improving relationship between his parents meant loss, and he ran away.

Once Paul and Janet would have used alcohol to alleviate the anxiety caused by such a crisis, and they would have acted independently instead of as a parental team, contradicting each other and increasing the confusion until one of the older children stepped into the vacuum. This time Paul was at work when Janet learned that Bob had run away. She turned to her AA sponsor; as she later explained, she wanted to be sure of getting support, and she didn't feel her relationship with Paul was strong enough for her to lean on him. She was afraid that this stressful situation might jeopardize her sobriety; if unsupported, she might regress to her old pattern of drinking to resolve problems.

The therapist framed this crisis as an opportunity for Paul and Janet to practice problem solving together. An emergency session was arranged with the couple so that they could discuss how they would deal with Bob when he returned.

For perhaps the first time in this couple's relationship, they were able to sit down together and make decisions about their children's problems. The therapist encouraged them to support each other without blaming themselves for the incident.

Alcoholics should not be pushed to take responsibility too soon. Experimenting with a new way of living, they have to learn to trust themselves and the people around them. In this situation, Janet, feeling the need of support, had turned to her AA sponsor instead of calling her husband. Paul was wounded, but after discussing the present state of their relationship with the therapist, he was able to accept Janet's fear of being let down by him. Thus the situation posed an opportunity not only for better functioning as parents but also for further progress in the spouse subunit.

Paul's reaction to Bob's running away had been rage. In the session with the spouses, the therapist helped him calm down and understand the dynamics of the incident. By running away, Bob was giving his family a message that he could not verbalize. Together, therapist and parents set a therapeutic goal. When Bob came back, they would help him verbalize his reasons for leaving home. The couple left the session feeling united and ready to deal with their son.

Bob was found in the evening, and a session was immediately arranged for the following morning. At the beginning of the session Bob was unable to talk, but after a while, with the help of the therapist and both his parents, he was able to say, "I had to go. There isn't enough room in the house for Daddy and me." The mood of the session changed; everybody was shocked, including the therapist. Paul's hurt was obvious on his face.

Everyone was silent for a few moments. Then Janet, facing Bob with a lot of difficulty, managed to say, "I need both of you. I care for both of you." This statement, coming on the heels of rejection by both his wife and son, brought tears to Paul's eyes. Watching his rigid father showing feeling and listening to his mother, Bob saw for perhaps the first time in his life that his parents were responsible and caring adults to whom he could talk. Everyone agreed that Bob must be helped to talk to his parents. The therapist also promised to alert Bob's Alateen sponsor to help Bob find age-appropriate peer group compensations for the necessary distancing from his mother.

Bob's difficulty talking to his parents was another direct result of their alcoholism. Children cannot experience a drunk adult as a rational, approachable, possible guide to help with problems in growing up. This therapeutic session may well have been Bob's first opportunity to talk to his mother and father.

He, like the other children, would have to learn that his parents were no longer incompetents to be protected but responsible adults who could help and guide them.

Later in therapy the focus shifted to Fred, who (the younger children reported) was drinking and smoking far too much. It unfortunately is common to find the children of alcoholics becoming alcoholics themselves. But the family focus in this case made preventive work possible. The fact that alcoholism was now discussed openly allowed Paul and Janet to share some of their own teenage experiences with drinking. Because his parents were able to share the memory of their emotions directly, these discussions had a profound effect on Fred.

The therapist urged the family to role-play a family scene in which drinking behavior had been present. This proved quite useful in helping the children share what they had experienced during the years when their parents were drinking and in making the parents realize the impact their behavior had had on their children.

At the same time, the Williams family had to learn to detach from alcoholism. When old behaviors were used and blamed on the time the parents were actively drinking, the therapist made the family aware that the alcoholism was not there anymore. The problem must be dealt with in new terms. Specifically Janet and Paul had to learn to support each other without blaming and to make demands on each other without the fear that making demands would drive the partner back to drinking. The children also had to learn to stop protecting both parents for fear of making them resume drinking.

After seven months of therapy, the Williams family decided to stop treatment. Paul and Janet were maintaining sobriety, and the family members all agreed that they felt comfortable with the changes that were happening. The therapist agreed with them but impressed on them the fact that help would always be available if the family felt unable to cope with further changes, including the normal changes that are part of every family's growth.

The treatment of the Williams family demonstrates many of the components of treating families affected by alcoholism.

Alcoholism has a profound effect on a family network, which must organize to compensate for the alcoholic's incapacity. Recovery from alcoholism is only a first step to the achievement of health for the system. The effectiveness of therapy can be maximal only if the social components of alcoholism and its consequences are corrected.

Paul and Janet Williams had taken the first, most difficult step for an alcoholic — working on their own drinking problems. Sobriety made them aware of their lack of leadership in the family. The children had assumed their roles: the oldest son was the disciplinary father; the middle son was the "mother's helper," the good boy; the youngest boy was still the baby, in his mother's bed. After the older sister left home, the youngest daughter felt lost and alone.

The therapist accepted a focus on reestablishing parental leadership. Change brought about a crisis when Bob, the youngest son, ran away. But the crisis gave the parents a chance to work together as a parental team and allowed the other children to experience a context in which feelings could be expressed and talked about without threat of punishment. As Bob stepped into the position of a "normal child," he also learned that he could express his feelings.

Some preventive work was accomplished when the subject of Fred's drinking came up. The family did not deny his problem; they discussed the issue in counseling and thought of ways to help Fred face the realities of being an alcoholic while he was still in an early stage.

Being together as parents also brought to the surface some of the good feelings that Paul and Janet had had in the past about each other. As individuals in early sobriety, they were also able to explore rebuilding their marriage in a healthy way without drinking. They will continue contact with AA to reinforce their personal growth.

4

~~~~~~~~~~

When Children Begin to Heal: *The Fitzpatricks*

Alcoholics often have genuine difficulty in recognizing anything abnormal about their behavior, particularly when their denial has persisted over a period of years. To this type of alcoholic, everyone else acts funny, or worse. Sometimes this perception that others need help can be used to bring the alcoholic to therapy.

I first met Pat Fitzpatrick at a group meeting on an alcoholism detoxification ward. Many such units hold daily group meetings in order to give an opportunity for ventilating feelings and/or for treatment. Meetings generally begin with complaints about the director, the nurse, the recreational facilities, and the food. Unhappiness is projected on the current environment. But in the process, the subject of alcohol use or abuse is brought up. Stories designed to elicit the group's sympathy are told, and the group usually responds profusely. In this supportive atmosphere, others begin to share their own unhappiness, and without the group's awareness, the meeting becomes first educational and then motivational. In the discussion of very personal complaints, participants may begin to think about what they could do for treatment.

One day a new man joined this particular group. He sat morosely in the corner, one eye blackened and one arm in a sling. It was Monday morning, rarely the happiest part of anyone's week, and the men gathering were grumbling more than usual as they sat down. Everyone seemed glum—restless after the weekend, with its decreased staff and curtailed activities. The griping became general.

Suddenly some remark seemed to touch a nerve in Pat. He sat up and began a bitter complaint about his wife. She was the crazy one. She should be locked up, not he.

The other men listened sympathetically as Pat protested the injustice of being committed by his crazy wife just because he had been beaten up in a bar. The group urged Pat to see that his wife got help. Everyone agreed that "crazy people have to be cared for." The group's support was crucial to Pat's willingness to enter therapy. The peer group helped him conceive therapy as a step to help his wife.

Hospital procedure required that Pat be psychiatrically evaluated. He cooperated, continuing to insist that his wife was the crazy one. The psychiatrist recommended that he join his wife in therapy, for her sake. This remark, coming on top of the group's discussion, helped him accept therapy.

We had learned that Pat, forty-three, lived with Mary, forty-one, and their daughter Gina, twenty-two, who had recently moved back with her parents after breaking up with her boyfriend. When I got in touch with Mary to arrange the first appointment, she stated angrily that she had committed Pat to a hospital specializing in alcoholism for two weeks' treatment and observation. "This time was the last straw," she said.

Questioning gently, I learned that Pat had been unemployed for months. Mary conceded that he did some of the household chores, but she seemed to see him as a bum living off his wife's and daughter's earnings. A few weeks ago, the family had decided to buy a used car; they all missed having one. Their credit rating was poor and they had no checking account, but Mary and Gina had scraped together $1,000 in cash and had given it to Pat so that he could choose the car. Pat had started out that morning with the cash and the best of intentions. But on his way to the auto dealership at 9 A.M. he had apparently decided to stop for a drink. Around 3:00 that afternoon the police had called Mary at work to tell her that Pat, heavily intoxicated, had been beaten up in the bar and required medical attention. Mary had found her husband with a black eye and a dislocated shoulder and without the $1,000, for which he was totally unable to account. Furious, Mary committed him to the detoxification unit of a center specializing in alcoholism.

Dostoevsky describes a similar scene in *Crime and Punishment:* " 'Gaolbird! Monster! . . . Where's the money? What have you got in your pockets? — show me!' . . . There was not a single kopek. 'Where is the money, then?' she cried. 'Oh, God, he can't have drunk it all! There were twelve silver roubles left in my box!' "

Mary said she was at the end of her rope. She only hoped the doctors would "straighten him out." But when I asked her to come to the hospital for a session and to bring Gina, she readily agreed.

The psychiatric resident asked me to join him as a cotherapist. This was taking a risk, because we did not know each other. But having met Pat on the ward and talked with Mary, I agreed to give it a try. To establish a closer cotherapist relationship, we agreed to meet before and after the session to establish therapeutic goals and to evaluate the transactions. Our earliest formulation was that, as a therapeutic team, we could model a couple negotiating conflicts for Pat and Mary.

Mary was a short, scrawny, plainly dressed woman with a sour expression. Gina's face was attractive, but she looked more like a fifteen-year-old than a college graduate. She was dressed like a teenager and was extremely shy. As soon as they entered the room, Mary and Gina sat close to each other. Pat sat on the opposite side of the room, close to the therapists, a spatial arrangement that turned out to be a very good picture of the family's organization.

Mary immediately began to rail at Pat. Words could not express the life she had led with this drunkard. The loss of all that money had only capped years of suffering. She demanded that the therapists make Pat "do something" about his drinking. Gina said nothing, but she grasped Mary's hand and glared at her father.

Pat did not remember the loss of the money, either because of a blackout or because his denial was so strong. He was totally bewildered by Mary's attack. Then he became furious. He still felt that Mary had violated his personal rights by committing him, and accusations flew back and forth. The couple was locked into an exchange of charges and countercharges that had virtually closed off any other aspect of their lives.

Gina anxiously watched her shouting parents. The therapists guessed that Gina, having broken up with her boyfriend, now felt trapped between her parents and roped into their problems. Each of the family members seemed at once overinvolved and estranged from the others. The two women needed help just as much as Pat did.

The therapists interrupted the marital quarrel to focus the session on plans for Pat's discharge from the hospital. This often turns out to be a helpful perspective. The technique makes the family look at an alcoholic as a sick person involved in a recovery process. There is hope of change but also recognition that change will not come overnight, anymore than recovery from any other serious illness. This task helps the family unite around a real issue.

Pat's physician had recommended Antabuse. Mary leapt on that point, insisting that Pat accept the prescription. That insurance that he would stop drinking was very important to her. Pat resisted, partly because of Mary's diatribe and partly because to him, taking Antabuse was a sign of weakness—that he was not man enough to handle his recovery. The therapists helped the couple negotiate a compromise. Pat would take the Antabuse, but Mary would not nag him about it, check up on him, or complain about his meeting his buddies at the neighborhood bar. This agreement was an important first step in rebuilding their relationship.

By the end of the first session several desirable therapeutic goals for this family became clear. An obvious first goal was alcoholism education. The Fitzpatricks had been living with the problems of alcoholism for twenty years but did not understand them or the emotional stress of living in an alcoholic situation. The therapists would have to help them think of alcoholism as an illness, see how this illness affected their lives, and learn to deal with it. The second goal would be rebuilding the marriage. Pat and Mary seemed to want to stay together, but they would have to work on their relationship. This would be important, too, for the third goal: setting Gina free from the triad.

Gina was a troubled young woman. She could not identify with her mother—a dissatisfied, bitter woman, or with her
father—an alcoholic unable to be father or husband. At the same
time, she was badly overinvolved in her parents' lives. She had
experienced living on her own, but she had come home to save
the family. Now that things were so bad at home, she could
not leave. Obviously she was in a trap.

The therapists and family agreed that Pat would enter
group therapy with the specific goal of working on his sobriety.
Pat and Mary resisted the idea of AA and Al-Anon ("It's *his*
problem," Mary snapped), but Pat felt comfortable with the idea
of group therapy. In addition, the threesome would continue in
family therapy, and several sessions would take place with Pat
and Mary alone to focus on marital issues.

Pat kept his commitment to take Antabuse and to work
on his drinking problem. Mary kept her end of the bargain,
and as Pat's functioning improved, so did their marriage. His
improving health also had important ramifications in their extended family. The Fitzpatricks lived in the same house with
Mary's parents, who occupied the first floor, and with her sister and brother-in-law, on the floor above. This arrangement,
not uncommon in ethnic groups where the importance of the
extended family is simply taken for granted, meant that Pat was
up against a formidable array of Italian in-laws with a family
bias against the Irish. As Pat's problems developed, Mary's
mother had repeatedly told her, "We warned you not to marry
that bum." Gradually Mary withdrew from her family because
of the shame of Pat's drinking. Pat's family, much more accepting
of drinking, tended to blame Mary for his problems. Thus Pat's
improvement made it possible for the couple to reestablish some
sorely missed ties to both sides.

As family sessions proceeded, Pat, Mary, and Gina started
to accept alcoholism as an illness, not as a weakness, and their
individual problems as family problems, not just as Pat's drinking. Next we addressed ourselves to specific steps designed to
help Gina separate from her parents' conflicts. She had a good
job, and with the therapists' encouragement and the reassurance

of her parents that they could take care of themselves, she made plans to move to her own apartment. Pat and Mary, now very aware of having overinvolved Gina in their lives, were careful to let her know that they would take care of their own problems in the future, seeking further couples therapy if necessary.

During this period, we held several sessions with Pat and Mary alone to discuss what they wanted in a husband-wife relationship. They began to work out some of the resentments of the past and in the process to build a new relationship that compensated for the vacuum created by Gina's leaving.

After three months, Gina had moved to her own apartment and had bought her own car. She had returned to graduate school and was dating a new boyfriend. Mary was beginning to depend on Pat, and he was able to give warmth and support and to accept it from her. They were developing outside activities that both enjoyed very much, so they no longer needed Gina as a daily part of their lives. We could see the change even in Mary's appearance.

At the end of six months the psychiatric resident left the hospital staff. A session was scheduled to discuss this development, and Gina was also invited. The therapists hardly recognized her. She was dressed like a woman her age, with a new hairstyle that set off her beautiful face. When the issue of continuing the sessons was brought up, Pat and Mary opted to terminate therapy. Pat was to continue in group therapy, and the couple felt they could integrate progress with their marriage without further help.

During this period the Fitzpatricks had acquired tools they had never known to help them work with conflict and to face problems in their family life in a more healthy way. We had the impression that we had opened a door and that these three people could now let themselves become part of the outside world.

Many children trapped in alcoholic families are afraid to leave home because they feel responsible for keeping the family together. In the Fitzpatrick family, accepting Pat's posing his wife as the sick member brought the family to treatment. It helped Pat accept his own problem with drinking and to work on it through group therapy. At the same time, as we looked at ways to improve the spousal relationship, we freed Gina from feeling responsible for keeping her parents together. Understanding the cultural background of this Italian and Irish family and educating the family about alcoholism lifted the sense of shame and made it possible for them to work on other areas of conflict in their lives.

5

Working with Family Subsystems: *The O'Briens*

A young adult alcoholic can sometimes be expressing his family's pathology by drinking. This case illustrates the life of one such man, who started individual treatment for alcoholism. The family was seen for a few exploratory sessions but family treatment proved unsuitable, and individual therapy continued as the treatment of choice.

Jack, age nineteen, was the older son of John and Alice O'Brien. John was a lawyer, and Alice was a teacher. Both functioned well in their professional lives. The younger son, Peter, was a high school student.

Now in college, Jack was having serious problems with excessive drinking. Concerned about the situation, Alice called an outpatient clinic that specialized in the treatment of alcoholism and made an appointment for her son. Jack met the therapist — a man not much older than himself — and developed a good relationship with him.

Jack had had his first drink at the age of nine, when his father took him to a bar to reward him for good grades in school. At age thirteen, he began drinking heavily, consuming a pint of whiskey and twelve cans of beer almost daily. Jack's mother called him schizophrenic; his father called him crazy; and his job supervisor at the college library called him an imbecile. Jack had always been taunted in the neighborhood and been labeled "queer" and "weirdo." He wanted to be a writer but said he could write only when drunk.

After evaluation, Jack decided to continue with the treatment offered, which implied a decision to stop drinking. The therapist suggested Antabuse as an adjunct to therapy, and Jack agreed to take it.

As soon as he stopped drinking, his functioning began to improve. Encouraged, the therapist decided to engage the family in treatment with the hope that this would accelerate Jack's recovery. Jack agreed somewhat reluctantly, and arrangements were made to have the whole family come to the agency. The therapist asked me to join him in a few exploratory family sessions as a consultant.

John O'Brien arrived at the agency at the set time, but Jack and his mother were twenty minutes late. They apologized, saying they had had trouble driving in the snow. Alice O'Brien immediately said that Peter was not coming because he had to attend some after-school activity.

As they were taking seats in the small room assigned for the session, the family plunged into a discussion of Jack's drinking. This was no surprise to the therapists; almost inevitably, alcoholism plays a central role in a family and their exchanges. Experience with alcoholism, however, does not necessarily teach people the facts about the problem or the way to deal with it. Both parents were rambling, mumbling abstractly about how destructive "drinking can be." Nothing positive was mentioned about Jack's accomplishment or his five months of sobriety. As in many families affected by alcoholism, Jack's problem was a scapegoat used to avoid discussing other problems in the family.

Jack became upset and complained that his parents were lecturing again. At home, his mother talked about his drinking all day long, and he hated it.

Strange as it may sound, Alice had arranged a party in the neighborhood pub to celebrate Jack's coming birthday. When Jack said he would like to have a mug of beer on his birthday, a family squabble developed. Alice O'Brien was clearly sending a double message: "You shouldn't, but you can."

The subject was dropped when John began to request information on how long the desire to drink persists in recovering alcoholics. Before the therapists could answer, the office phone rang. It was Peter, asking to speak to his mother or father immediately. Alice picked up the phone, listened, and said she could not attend to him now because she was involved in the session. She asked him why, if he was home already, he had said he would be too busy to come to the session. Then we heard her resisting Peter's request to speak to John, though she finally acquiesced and handed the receiver to her husband. John spoke abruptly to him and said he could not spend time on the phone now and hung up. Mother and Jack were watching and listening attentively.

After John hung up, Jack said tearfully that Peter's excuse was not true. He just did not want to become involved; he did not care about Jack's therapy. Alice defended Peter, stating angrily that Peter had always been concerned about Jack. She said he had taken an active role in throwing away Jack's whiskey as well as insisting on the importance of getting Jack into treatment. Peter, she said, had suffered so much, the poor boy, and he had never made her run to the neighbors, "hat in hand." Jack was overwhelmed with fury.

Alice continued defending Peter. John interrupted, as if totally unaware of Jack's reaction, to comment cheerfully on Peter's "Freudian reaction formations" in his manner of showing love toward Jack.

The therapists, responding to Jack's anger, tried to stop both parents and to make them aware of him. Jack was raging, demanding that his mother talk about "hat in hand." For the last few days, he said, he had been thinking about taking a drink just to show his family.

This was a crucial element to understanding the dislocation of thinking in the family system. It seemed that even extreme anger bounced off Jack's parents. Only his drinking attracted their attention.

Alice began to talk, with a voice devoid of emotion, about Jack's problems as a child. She said that he had been hyperactive. She had studied everything related to Jack's condition that was then available. John shrugged and sat back, tuning out his wife's monologue. Jack calmed down until Alice got off the track and began talking about Peter and how she became so absorbed working with Jack that Peter was ignored.

Jack grew increasingly upset as she talked about his brother. He began to complain about Peter, saying he was constantly terrorized by him. Jack said he could never get his own way when Peter was around. John sat up straight and supported Jack, saying that Alice always defended Peter even in the worst aspects of his behavior. Father seemed to be strongly allied with Jack; in fact, he was fighting his wife through Jack.

Feeling supported, Jack began to give examples of how his brother terrorized him. He said Peter used to change channels when he was watching a TV program. Alice ignored his complaints and said that Peter had lacked experiences in life, whereas Jack had had everything—even a trip to Europe. In fact, Jack was now dating the girl who had been Peter's girlfriend. She continued on the same track, talking about Peter's deprivations.

Suddenly Jack exploded, screaming furiously that he wanted his mother to tell us about this "hat in hand." Everything always revolved around Peter, he complained. Even now she was getting off the track, talking about Peter. He was sick of it.

Alice was startled and said she did not know what Jack wanted. The exchange continued, Jack demanding that his mother go on with the "hat in hand" business and Alice feigning no knowledge of it. Finally, when Jack persisted, she explained to the therapists that the expression referred to the time when the parents in the neighborhood had contacted her, complaining that Jack was involved in an adolescent homosexual situation. She had had to go running, "hat in hand," she said, to defend him. The question arose: had Jack been in difficulty even before his drinking started?

John joined Jack and intimated for the first time that his wife did not allow him to act as a father to Peter. Jack screamed that he resented all the talk about Peter. Alice resumed her narrative about her struggles to raise Jack. At that point, John said that Jack had been brutalized as a young child in school because of his eccentric behavior and his interest in stamps. This engaged John in a fight with the school administration on his son's behalf.

The open alliance between John and Jack may have been

too much for Alice. She drew the therapists' attention to herself, saying that she had something painful she wanted to say. She often felt, she said, that she had three sons. Her husband always came to her to make decisions about the boys. He complained about Peter to her instead of dealing with his son himself.

Alice's behavior at this point was a repetition of a family pattern the therapists had noted before. Whenever one member of this family began to relate to another—John defending Jack, in this case—a third member entered, interrupting the first two by bringing up different problems.

Now Alice continued her complaints. When Peter was born, she said, John had said he felt he had just gained a "brother." John, somewhat embarrassed, growled, "What's wrong with that?" Alice answered that she felt dissatisfied as a woman. John retorted defensively that he felt dissatisfied as a man.

The focus of the session seemed to be veering toward the couple. They began attacking each other, but Jack interrupted, not allowing his parents to interact. Again the pattern of this family emerged: a dyadic interchange generally interrupted by the entrance of a third.

Because the agency allowed no flexibility in scheduling, the session had to end at this point. The therapists felt overwhelmed by the mass of information and the chaotic way this family communicated. But they encouraged the family to return for another session, and they agreed.

John, Alice, and Jack arrived together for the second session. Peter was not with them, and again Alice explained apologetically that Peter was not coming. This had been a shock, she said. She had felt sure that Peter would come this time. Jack said he had felt sure Peter would not come.

Peter's absence threatened to become the focus again, but the therapists interrupted, suspecting the "absent member maneuver." The O'Briens were asked whether Peter's absence was planned. Were they avoiding other issues by focusing on the family member who was not here? The family was silent for a moment. When it became clear that no answer would be given, the therapists said the session must continue without talking about Peter.

After a moment Alice began, saying that Jack had criticized

her after the last session for not giving the neurological details of his childhood problems. Now she began to talk about that in great detail. The therapist asked, "Why do you have to do what Jack says?" Alice stated that she had to "serve her family." Then she moved to the present. She expressed great concern about Jack, who had been extremely depressed last Friday night. Jack jumped in angrily to say that he was tired of his mother's concern. He immediately began a lengthy discussion of his history teacher's grading practices, and both parents encouraged him to talk about this in great detail. The therapists asked Jack to tell more about his Friday night depression. They felt themselves falling into the family's confusion, but they still attempted to make Jack tell more specifically about what his mother had called "depression." In working with families affected by alcoholism, the therapist must always be alert to mood changes in the alcoholic member and to any hint of relapse or family cover-up.

John intervened, saying that Jack had had an "Antabuse reaction," and slowly the story unfolded. Jack, drinking in his room on Friday evening, had developed an Antabuse reaction (a rash, hot flashes, and difficulty breathing). John said he had been concerned about his son, so he had driven him to work that night. The family had not even considered calling a doctor, however, ignoring the potentially serious medical effects of an Antabuse reaction.

The therapist showed concern about the incident, stressing how the three of them intellectualized tremendously about everything, dwelling on academic matters while ignoring serious here-and-now problems. Alice changed the subject and tried to talk about having to satisfy everybody. John said the family was slipping into a situation where the children ruled the parents. He expressed hopelessness about any possibility of change and intense feelings of resentment toward Peter. Jack, becoming annoyed, tried to talk again about his history teacher. Alice began talking about Peter. The session grew chaotic; in fact, the confusion was even worse than in the first session. What therapeutic strategy could have succeeded then? The therapists felt almost lost and at this point in the session expressed their confusion and asked the family to deal with one issue at a time.

Starting with the father, they asked John to share what was happening to him. Accusations began again, and once again an intense argument was raging. Everybody was talking at once; the only people listening were the therapists. An attempt was made to end the session with an emphasis on the seriousness of Jack's Antabuse reaction and their concern about Jack's relapse, but the family could not listen.

After the session, the therapists met for a conference. Was family treatment the best approach in this case? Or should the goal be to free Jack, at age nineteen, from this environment and to help him in individual therapy gain independence without drinking? No contract for family treatment had been agreed on, and the agency was not equipped with emergency services. A crisis undoubtedly could have been created to confront this family with the need for a change, but the therapists were far from certain that this was the correct course.

The question was still unresolved a few days later when Jack's therapist received a phone call from Alice, who said that Jack would be late for his appointment but was on the way. When he arrived, Jack had a glazed look on his face, his eyes were red, and his breath smelled of beer. As soon as he sat down, he began talking hysterically. Jack was drunk, and the therapist interrupted to tell him so. Jack whispered that he was going to tell the therapist something personal that must not come up in the family sessions: he had been drinking three to four beers a day for the last five days. The therapist questioned about the Antabuse; Jack replied that he had been slipping the pills through his fingers every morning.

The session immediately focused on the drinking, the therapist directly confronting Jack with his condition. Basically he told Jack that he must take responsibility for stopping drinking; drinking was jeopardizing every area of his life.

Jack's reply was an incoherent ramble about his intense fears; unable to focus on any issue, he merely avoided the question of drinking. The therapist told him that they could talk more about these other issues at some other time, when Jack was sober. At the moment, however, the concern was for the immediate problems: how was Jack going to get himself home safely? How would he stop drinking and start on Antabuse again? The therapist also pointed out that Jack should discuss his feelings about family sessions during a family session. If the O'Briens wanted to stop family sessions, this should be a joint decision.

Jack seemed helpless and confused, but he showed considerable trust. He accepted the therapist's suggestion that he go straight home and rest. The therapist encouraged Jack to call him the next day and to tell him how he was doing.

How best to handle a situation like this is a debatable issue. Some therapists would insist on seeing the family together while the patient is intoxicated. Others would work with the alcoholic alone, helping him sober up, and then continue family treatment. Still others would deal immediately with some of the intense feelings brought up by the patient. In Jack's case, the therapists decided on the second strategy, and it was suggested that Mr. and Mrs. O'Brien come for a few couple sessions while Jack was recuperating from his relapse. They agreed to come at the time originally scheduled for family sessions.

But the couple session proved to be a repetition of the family sessions. Each spouse reported the history of his or her life. In quiet, factual style, both related episodes and symptoms that indicated significant pathology. But they touched on their relationship only in complaining to the therapist about each other.

Was this family ready for changes? Or was only the pathology of each member keeping them all together? If changes were brought about, would the family members collapse?

During this period, Peter arrived unannounced one morning, asking to see Jack's therapist. Surprised but curious to know what had brought him, the therapist saw him. In spite of Jack's descriptions of their infantile bickering, Peter proved to be a tall, quite bright fifteen-year-old. He conducted himself in an effeminate and artificially adult manner. As he shook the therapist's hand, he announced that he was "reporting" on behalf of his brother and would be glad to tell anything that could be helpful. He denied having any problems of his own. Rather romantically, he spoke about the fine oak paneling of his family's home and his fondness for antiques. He mentioned briefly his love for the theater and his plans to study acting. Finally he announced that he had no intention of coming for treatment sessions, at which point the therapist merely thanked him for coming in.

We never learned why Peter decided to show up. Perhaps he sensed harbingers of change in the family. Had changes occurred that the therapists were unaware of?

Each member of the O'Brien family exhibited serious problems, and the family structure was pathogenic. Yet each member seemed to be functioning well in the extrafamilial world. The father held a professional job and was accepted in his field. So too was the mother at her work. Peter had his life mapped out. Jack had established a good relationship with the individual therapist and was ready to continue treatment.

Exploratory family sessions had clarified some aspects of family structure, and therapeutic possibilities could have been mapped out. But the only way to create real change in this family would have been to push them into crisis. A definite possibility was that the result would be four people institutionalized, perhaps for life.

An alternative plan was decided on. Jack would continue his efforts to keep himself from drinking, and individual sessions would determine what changes could be accomplished in other areas of his life. Soon he would have to move out of the family, which would free him from having to act out all the family's problems.

In conclusion, the O'Briens are an example of a family for which family therapy was not appropriate. In the end, it was decided that since the family was functioning after a fashion and family members were doing well in the outside world, it was best not to try to force change at that time. In a sense, we decided to let the O'Briens continue functioning crazily at home but well in the outside world. Sometimes therapists must make this decision. Since Jack was willing to continue in individual therapy, we would leave well enough alone with the rest of the family.

As children grow up, they are expected to develop lives of their own. But we know that many carry unresolved issues from their family of origin. In Jack's case, the therapist's decision to continue on an individual basis was made for the purpose of helping Jack work on many of these unresolved issues. This change in approach was not implemented to alienate Jack from his family. If Jack accepts his individuality, he will be able to be part of his family without falling into the role and behavior patterns of the past.

Young Jack accepted his mother's suggestion to initiate treatment for his drinking problem. The relationship with his therapist, a young man almost his age, helped him concentrate and work on the problem. He did not join a self-help group but continued in individual therapy.

6

~~~~~~~~~~~~~

Uncovering
Family Collusions:
The Giacomellis

When a woman does not work outside the home, alcoholism can often be hidden for years, with the collusion of the family. In such cases, the family becomes as much a part of the denial as the alcoholic member herself. Uncovering and confronting the alcoholism as an issue may require a massive family intervention, and this in turn may create a serious crisis.

The Giacomellis entered treatment when Mr. Giacomelli called a mental health center to request help for his wife, who was suffering from nearly immobilizing depression. At the time, the center was experimenting with a new procedure whereby families were required to come with patients to the initial interview. Arrangements were made to see the Giacomelli family as a unit. Present in the session were Tony, thirty-nine; Anina, thirty-eight; Carmela, sixteen; Jack, fourteen; Don, twelve; and Julian, six.

The central focus was Anina's depression. Everyone agreed that she was the problem. She could not keep up with the housework, and every afternoon when the children came home from school they found her lying on the couch, suffering from one of her severe headaches. She could no longer participate in most family and community activities, to the point that it had become a severe problem to the family. They all wanted to see a change. Father and the three older children continued talking in terms of "depression," but Julian, reluctantly but determinedly, called the therapist's attention to himself.

"I can tell you what's been happening since I was born," he told her. "For anything before that, you'll have to ask the others." The therapist encouraged Julian to talk. "There's always a glass next to her," Julian said. "And sometimes she doesn't walk straight."

Now that the cat was out of the bag, everyone felt free to talk about Anina's drinking. The whole family knew that she was not suffering from headaches; she was intoxicated every afternoon. Episode after episode about her erratic behavior at home was recounted; everyone had an anecdote to contribute. The family kept the mood light. Sometimes even Anina laughed. But to find out that the whole family knew she drank was a severe shock to her.

The session focused on family members' experiences with Anina's drinking and how deeply it had affected everyone. They felt isolated from extended family and friends. Carmela complained that she never felt free to go out with her friends. She had to come straight home from school to tidy the house and start dinner. On weekends she left the house only when she knew her father would be home. Jack said he, too, tried to get home from school right away, and he complained about Don, who stayed out until supper time, ate, and immediately went out again. Tony explained that his work required long hours but that in the evening, he helped Carmela finish the chores. Julian, the baby, was always playing one parent against the other and was growing quite spoiled as a result.

The family members began to complain about each other, each feeling that the other could do more. They all made it plain that it was Anina's role they were trying to fill, but none of them confronted her directly. It was obvious that Anina would have to deal with her drinking problem by herself. The therapist made an appointment with Anina and Tony for the next day. They agreed that it would be important to get a good history of Anina's drinking before formulating any plans for treatment. The first step was already taken: identification of alcoholism as Anina's and the family's problem. Subsequently the task would come of removing it from its central position as the family's curse. It was agreed that family sessions would also be scheduled.

Because Anina reacted positively during the session and made a commitment to work out her problem, the Giacomellis felt sure she could control the situation until the next day. But

that evening Anina smuggled a fifth of whiskey into the bath-
room, drank most of it, and tried to cut her wrists. She had
to be rushed to the emergency room, and from there she was
admitted to a detoxification unit.

The therapist visited Anina at the detoxification unit.
Anina was angry, resentful, and remorseful. Although she had
been hospitalized before for various symptoms, she had never
before been admitted acutely intoxicated. She hated being "in
with all these drunks," and she blamed the therapist for reveal-
ing a secret she insisted no one had known about until now. On
the therapist's second visit, Anina, detoxified and clearheaded,
was able to see things more realistically, and she greeted the
therapist in a friendly way.

Anina was extremely surprised at this second visit — she
was amazed that the therapist had considered her worth one
subway ride, let alone two. "Why are you so nice to me?" she
asked. As with so many alcoholics, she did not seem to feel she
was worth the time of a busy professional. The therapist answered simply that she was concerned about Anina and wanted
to see her when she was not under the influence of alcohol.

Feeling accepted, Anina suddenly began to unwind and
to open up. She talked about her drinking history, the shame
of being an alcoholic in a family of "good" people, the years of
fear and concealment and ever-increasing dependence. She had
started to drink shortly after Julian's birth because she was feeling
"more and more nervous" — isolated and unable to cope with a
household of four active children. A doctor whom she consulted
prescribed tranquilizers, and she took them as well. But more
and more often, she had found that drinking calmed her down.
Now she felt trapped. Her husband was having an affair; he
did not love her anymore, and who could blame him? The
children all were unhappy, and it was her fault. No one could
help — all the doctors ever did was write more prescriptions. At
that point, she got out of bed and went to her suitcase, where
she had hidden her pocketbook. She opened it, and it contained
enough prescription bottles to stock a medicine chest.

The therapist held out her hand. Anina understood and
handed her the pocketbook. "Keep these for me?" she pleaded.

The therapist said that she would and began to discuss

future plans with Anina, who was to be discharged the next day. Therapy must begin immediately. Sessions would be held with the entire family and with Anina and Tony alone, but the priority was to work on Anina's drinking problem. Anina hesitated, mentioning "depression" and "possible change-of-life symptoms," but the therapist was firm: the focus must be on alcoholism; that was the central problem. Anina finally agreed.

In some cases it is the patient's own determination to do something about the alcoholism problem that finally facilitates successful treatment. But many times confronting the problem can be initiated by a therapist who shows care and respect for the person's worth while insisting that the problem be dealt with. In Anina's case, her suicide attempt exerted a positive influence. Anina became deeply troubled by the fact that she had been so threatened by the prospect of life without drinking that she had tried to cut her wrists. With the therapist's encouragement, she determined to try to find a way out of this trap.

The session the next day included the entire family. The focus was future plans. It was agreed that the main target would be Anina's drinking and that she would take care of that. But the rest of the family would also begin to look at possible changes indicated by the issues brought up in the first session. The family accepted the therapist's advice to treat Anina like any other patient recuperating after a period of hospitalization. As Anina regained strength, family sessions would help her resume her tasks and change her position in the family organization.

Anina was referred to AA, but she never felt comfortable with that group. She was much more comfortable with a therapy group of women alcoholics run by the same therapist. This eventually became a strong network of support not only for her drinking problem but also for building her self-esteem.

As Anina began to gain strength through individual and group sessions, the therapist scheduled couple sessions. In one session she encouraged Anina to discuss her resentment of Tony. Anina knew perfectly well that he had been experimenting with extramarital relationships, but this had never been mentioned between them. Now she took the opportunity, and Tony began to tell his side. As soon as the area was opened, Anina began to understand how much her drinking, which had made her unavailable as a wife, had contributed to his search for extra-marital warmth and companionship. Winning her husband back began to seem a direct reward for changing, and she set to work with renewed determination.

Tasks designed to encourage the development of support and intimacy within the spouse unit were assigned, and both Anina and Tony moved quickly to find almost-forgotten gratifications within that relationship.

For women alcoholics, the integration of their growth in a spousal relationship becomes more difficult as alcoholism progresses. A husband who at first found it fun to have sex with an intoxicated woman who allowed anything may eventually learn not to expect any rewarding response. He may deny his own sexual needs or sacrifice them for the sake of his impaired wife.

Recovery can also pose significant problems. A recovering woman may become more conscious of her own sexuality. In some cases her husband may find new demands in the relationship that he is not prepared to supply. In other cases he may feel frustrated and impatient at having to wait while his wife adjusts to her new self-image. If the husband has been having an affair, this is often brought into the open at this stage. In other families the alcoholic's partner may begin an affair as the alcoholic begins to recover. Many couples separate or divorce at this time.

One of Anina's main problems was her sense of failure as a mother and a housewife. In her patriarchal Italian neighborhood, in the midst of a house-proud, upwardly mobile, working-class family, she had felt her lack of contribution keenly.

Alcoholic women in recovery must reinforce self-esteem and self-worth as a person before functioning in expected female roles. They must feel fulfilled and derive satisfaction for themselves before they can start to provide support for others. If they do fill other roles, in many cases it is because of family expectations, not because they are ready.

Some clinical data show that women alcoholics are more likely to have affective disorders, depression, marital instability, and lower self-esteem. Many have been sexually abused. Patterns of heavy drinking develop at life crisis situations. Accordingly, in some cases specialized programs for alcoholic women are recommended to take care of some of these other problems at the same time they address the alcoholism.

In Anina's case, however, tasks were assigned to return her to the role she saw as hers. For example, she was instructed to eat with the family—something she had almost stopped doing during the drinking years. Soon she began to take on the responsibility for cooking and cleaning. Carmela was to help her, but Anina was in charge. Gaining more and more confidence, Anina began to take over once more, freeing Carmela and the other children to go out with their friends and to lead a normal teenage life. Julian, no longer able to play one parent against the other, also began to grow out of his infantile stance and to develop into an outgoing, tough grade-schooler.

As Tony and Anina pulled closer together, they also began to establish better functioning as parents. Together they set rules, and together they enforced them. They were concerned about their children; the picture presented in the first session seemed to be confirmed by their descriptions. Carmela was a little mother, Jack was the good older son, Don was an outsider, rebelling and acting out, and Julian was Anina's baby. It was a pattern often seen in alcoholic families.

With the therapist's help, Tony and Anina began to practice acting as a unified parental team in the sessions. Homework assignments continued their practice during the week. This helped them use their new strength as a couple to firm up the family foundation.

Unfortunately, Anina's rapid return to competence had forced Carmela into a shatteringly quick role shift. The boys, close to a competent father, had never been quite so badly affected by Anina's disability, but Carmela had taken over as mother and housekeeper in a family with no other girls. Therapist and parents discussed ways of helping her shed responsibility and find compensation in her extended family and peer group, but before much could be done, Carmela became pregnant.

Though they were both still in high school, Carmela was adamant: she and her boyfriend must get married. They did, and both dropped out of school. Unable to envision herself in any other role in life, Carmela had engineered a rapid movement into the position of mother of a family of her own.

Tony and Anina both felt Carmela was too young to marry. Several sessions were held to help the family discuss the matter, and finally they agreed to the marriage. Therapy had helped them build up the strength to cope together with this family crisis. But the Giacomellis felt so disgraced that they decided to move to another city. Therapy had to be terminated when they moved, about six months after initiation.

Anina's improvement in therapy had been dramatic. It showed even in her physical appearance, as she began to take care of herself again. For Tony, Anina, and probably the boys, the results were excellent. For Carmela, her mother's improvement had been too rapid.

If therapy had continued, the mother-daughter subsystem would have become a focus. It would have been important to help Anina reach out to her daughter, to help her feel like a daughter again instead of the mother and housekeeper of the family. Unfortunately, the speed at which Anina resumed her roles pushed Carmela out of the family, toward a family of her own. One could only hope that in the future, circumstances would open her life to the opportunities her mother's drinking had closed off during her adolescence.

The family session that opened Pandora's box to Anina's alcoholism also helped the family reach out for help when Anina overdosed herself with whiskey and cut her wrists. Bringing her alcoholism into the open allowed Anina to work on it, especially in an alcoholic women's group run by the female therapist with whom she had developed a trusting relationship.

Anina's desire to become a healthy wife and mother changed the family structure. The children could be children again as the parents took on parental roles. Through the group, Anina developed confidence in herself, and when the crisis of Carmela's pregnancy came up, she used the support of the group and did not have to resort to drinking.

The therapist, however, should have seen early in treatment the possibility of Carmela's looking for a way to continue the role she had been playing. An individual or adolescent therapy group might have given her the support and confidence to grow out of her role of pseudomother and wife and to enjoy her adolescent years.

7

Misreading
a Problem Child:
The Richardsons

Alcoholism in a parent can have a devastating effect on a child, who may entirely lack the security of knowing that his needs will be provided for. If such a child comes to the attention of a therapist, he may be misread, leading to a situation in which therapy focuses on presumed faults within the child instead of the lack of stability in his most vital context.

When Peter Richardson was ten, his school referred him to the pediatric department of a nearby hospital. Peter's teachers complained that he was hyperactive, unable to concentrate or to keep still. He also presented severe reading problems. With these symptoms, the obvious course was to have Peter evaluated by a child psychiatrist, who made a diagnosis of early schizophrenia. Peter began individual therapy and remedial reading classes.

The hospital was organized in the traditional way whereby a psychiatrist worked with the child and a social worker saw the family in auxiliary therapy. An appointment was made with Peter's mother, Collette.

The first meeting was scheduled for 11 A.M. As the social worker shook hands with Collette, she smelled liquor on her breath. Without embarrassment and with a very comfortable attitude, she asked Collette whether she had been drinking before coming to the session. Collette, surprised by the social worker's directness, admitted with some embarrassment that she had had to have a drink before coming.

The story of the Richardsons began to unfold. Collette had been drinking heavily since her late teens, and presently

78

she was unable to control her alcohol intake. As she spoke about herself, she also revealed that her husband, Sean, was an active alcoholic. The session shifted from a focus on Peter "the schizophrenic" to a concentration on drinking problems.

The social worker decided to work with both parents in cooperation with the alcoholism division of the hospital. The first step was to see whether Collette and Sean were willing to look into the problem. Both agreed, and furthermore, Sean agreed to be hospitalized for detoxification. Collette, with the therapist's support, was able to stop drinking without medical intervention. Both were referred to AA, though Sean became more involved than Collette.

As the parents' functioning improved, they began to look into the organization of the family. Peter, too, was showing improvements, and the therapist, greatly encouraged, arranged for the Richardsons to be seen as a family. Sean had been sober during this period, though he was still unemployed and in poor health. Collette had recovered enough to hold a job, but she could remain sober only for a few weeks at a time and then she would relapse.

As soon as information on the Richardsons became available to the family therapy team, it became obvious that Peter, diagnosed as an early schizophrenic by an individual therapist because of wildly erratic behavior, was actually a barometer of his parents' functioning. Peter was Collette's son by her first marriage; he had never known his own father. Collette had married Sean in a drunken stage when Peter was two. All his life, the child had lived with two active, heavy drinkers. Drunkenness was the normal life-style of this family; Peter did not know people could live any other way. Without friends, he spent his time in the apartment, watching TV, with the dog for company. Often he was the one who called the local liquor store for a delivery. When his mother was functioning well, Peter would begin to do better in school, to keep his appointments with the psychiatrist, and to attend his remedial reading classes. As soon as his mother started drinking again, his functioning would become "schizophrenic."

When family therapy began, Sean was the outsider in the

family. He had been sober for six months, but he kept himself busy with AA activities from early evening until late at night and then slept until noon, unable to mobilize himself for any other activity. Collette was working, but she had become a chain smoker and was now in a stage of denial about her drinking. As she saw it, she occasionally took a drink or two. She thought she could control her drinking and remain a social drinker, an idea not borne out by her past history.

Both parents came from wealthy families. Sean had a Ph.D. with honors from a prestigious university, but he had never been able to practice his profession. Collette had been educated at an exclusive school and had once tried a career as a dancer. They both had run through their inheritances, and the family was now on welfare plus whatever Collette earned as a temporary secretary during her periods of sobriety.

The family history showed that Collette had the capacity to quit drinking without medication or hospitalization, but she would always start again. Sean, though now sober for six months, was immobilized by the long years of drinking. He showed no self-esteem and no capacity to feel or express emotion. Nevertheless, both parents saw Peter as the sick member of the family. They came to family therapy only in an effort to help their son. Very discouraged by the diagnosis of early schizophrenia, they were afraid that nothing could be done for Peter.

By the second family session, it was time to arrange summer camp for Peter. He was afraid to leave home, terrified that his mother would die while he was away. Because it was necessary to pull the therapeutic team together, a session with Peter's psychiatrist, the social worker, the remedial reading teacher, and the family therapists was arranged.

Peter was unusually restless during the session, lying on the floor most of the time and repeatedly recounting the experience of a child he had heard of who went to camp and who had received a letter saying his mother had died. Neither his parents nor the therapists were able to calm Peter down or even to get him to sit in a chair.

How could Peter be reassured? We suggested that Collette keep in touch with him, and she promised to send him a postcard at camp every day.

The therapists were concerned about the outcome, knowing that Collette was still drinking off and on. It was a difficult session, too, for Peter's psychiatrist, who was psychoanalytically oriented. It turned out that sharing their experience with a group of professionals was reassuring to the parents. It was decided that Sean and Collette would continue therapy as a couple while Peter was away. The plan proceeded, Peter went to camp, and Collette kept her promise to write him daily.

Unfortunately, the Richardsons still insisted on believing that Peter was the sick family member. They could not progress further to the point of dealing with the problems in their own relationship, and Sean could not be brought to focus on his relationship with his stepson. It was amazing how available they were to treatment but how difficult it was for them to see that any change in themselves was necessary. It seemed that they would come to sessions willingly and indefinitely as long as the subject was only Peter's condition.

When Peter returned from camp, the Richardsons were referred to a multifamily group then being formed. A *multifamily group* is a "hybrid" of family therapy and group therapy, according to Laqueur (1968). Like family therapy, its target is the dysfunctioning family system, but it is a method that allows feedback from a *suprasystem* — the outside world as represented by other families. In multifamily therapy, roles in the single family tend to diffuse through cross-family interaction. Problem members are different in every family, so a child with a drinking father, for instance, can relate in the multifamily group to a better-functioning father from another family. In addition, observation of how other families function can provide modeling for members of the group.

The goals of multifamily therapy are

1. To decrease denial via sharing and identification
2. To help "well" family members identify themselves as part of the homeostatic functioning of the family

3.   To develop problem-solving skills through the use of other
     group members as sounding boards and as modelers of
     different skills

   In the group the Richardsons agreed to join, two of the
families had children Peter's age. Alcoholic parental dysfunctioning was present in some of the other families, but the Johnson family had a strong father who saw himself as his sons' chief
disciplinarian. Along with his authority, he had the capacity
to guide and to communicate warmth. The therapists hoped that
Mr. Johnson could become Peter's surrogate father and influence
his behavior. It was also possible that the group would be able
to break through Collette's denial of her alcoholism, confronting her from the perspective of people in the same boat.
   The multifamily group gave Peter siblings and the figure
of a strong father who could also be a model for Sean. When
Peter became restless, Mr. Johnson could help him set controls.
The Johnson boys, both bright, healthy children, discussed life
situations with Peter and helped him face them in a more realistic
way. In one session, for example, the children began to discuss
sex. Peter had been sexually used by some men in the local park.
He told of his experiences, expressing his confusion and hurt.
The Johnsons helped him talk about it, and Peter was able to
work through the problem with the help of the adults and children in the group.
   For the first time, we felt that Peter was moving toward
genuine improvement. He was relating to people, speaking when
spoken to, and beginning to be more relaxed. The multifamily
group gave him a family context and showed him care and understanding.
   Unfortunately, Sean's passive approach to life continued,
and Collette still had ups and downs with her drinking. Furthermore, the family had lost its identified patient, and the
Richardsons started to feel the pressure to look at what they
were doing themselves. Without warning, Collette had a bad
relapse, and this time Sean started to drink again. Soon the situation was entirely out of control, with both parents intoxicated
and unreachable and Peter staying home from school and ses-

sions in order to help keep the household together. The old style of life returned. The therapists, the Johnsons, and Sean's AA sponsor all tried without success to reach the family to persuade the parents to take steps toward detoxification.

The professional team decided on a home visit. Peter let the therapist in. The apartment was a shambles. Both parents were intoxicated and semiclothed, Sean lying on the bed and Collette on the couch. The team had to make a decision. They agreed that Peter must be removed from the house, for his own protection and in the hope of creating a therapeutic crisis for this family. Peter left with the therapist.

As soon as Peter was gone, Collette admitted herself for detoxification. Sean called his AA fellows. They came over, helped him clean the apartment, and then took him to the hospital's detoxification unit. As the therapists had hoped, the crisis mobilized the Richardsons to stop drinking. But Collette resented the fact that her son had been removed while she lay intoxicated. Two days later she picked up Peter at the shelter on her way home from the detoxification unit. She refused to have any further contact with the therapeutic team.

How can this case be evaluated? For Peter, the results were good — we know this because he continued with remedial reading classes and we were able to follow his progress with his teacher. In the combination of individual, family, and family group treatment, Peter had learned that life can be different — that families can be organized around something other than drinking and fighting. His remedial reading teacher felt that he was integrating this experience into his life and that his continuing good relationship with her was another positive experience for this child. The prognosis for Peter's parents was more guarded. Sean had become actively involved in AA and had had some success in maintaining sobriety. He might soon be ready to focus on himself, though it seemed it would be some time before he had the strength to pick up the roles of husband, father, and provider. For Collette, the prognosis was the poorest. Though she now saw her drinking as a problem in the family, she had not accepted the fact that she must deal with it by stopping her alcohol intake. I met her some six years later at a different agency, still unenthusiastically "seeking help" for her "drinking problem."

The label of "problem child" was removed from Peter. He began to accept a new self-image, which will be reinforced in his individual therapy. If possible, family sessions may supplement the individual sessions. If necessary, the professional team will help him find healthy role models outside his home.

The crisis created by removing Peter from the home while his parents were drunk was the breaking point for possible changes in the therapeutic approach.

The future of Sean and Collette remains questionable. As we know, some alcoholics, after attempting many different treatments, recover and manage to live seminormal lives. The heavy drinking of past years, however, could leave serious physical problems. Knowing the situation of these two individuals makes it difficult to predict the future.

8

Is Sobriety Enough?
The Harrisons

Exchanges within the alcoholic family develop "around" the skew caused by the alcoholic member's incapacity. Even if the latter attains sobriety, the patterns established over the drinking years may continue to hamper individual and family development unless family members become aware of the need for change.

Fred and Clara Harrison came to therapy after hearing me deliver a talk at a combined AA and Al-Anon meeting about "communication in the family." Fred, age forty-four, was an alcoholic who had succeeded in maintaining sobriety for five years with the help of AA. He held a responsible job at an export firm and was very involved with the AA program. Clara worked as an executive secretary, was attending night school, and was equally involved with Al-Anon. When she called for an appointment, she expressed dissatisfaction with her life. She could not elaborate much further besides indicating that my talk had made her aware of a "lack of communication" in her family and between Fred and her.

A meeting with the couple was arranged. After the usual social chitchat, I asked the Harrisons to describe their relationship. Clara immediately began to complain about the lack of contact between her and Fred and then continued with a description of the family at present. Clara saw herself as being away from home most of the time, busy with work, school, and Al-Anon. She spent her lunch hours in a bookstore; at home, she read. Mary, age twenty, did most of the housework, took care of the family, and was taking some college courses part-time.

Rosalie, age twenty-one, was just back from a long vacation in Europe. Freddie, age nineteen, had dropped out of college and was in the process of looking for a job. He was very disoriented about his future.

Clara paused, and Fred began to talk about himself. He was busy working and very much involved with AA, where he was sponsoring several young men. At home, he took care of some of the household chores. His particular job was to go shopping with Mary on Saturday morning so that Clara could sleep late.

This brought the couple back to Clara's initial statement that the two of them did very little together. It seemed that during the drinking years, the Harrison family had developed the not uncommon pattern of allowing the children to take on the tasks of the drinking parent, as well as those of the overburdened nondrinking parent. This pattern, persisting for years, had seemed normal to the Harrisons. But now several things were happening and Clara, at age forty-three, was facing significant changes in her life. They were negotiating the purchase of a new house, which would mean a move away from Clara's mother, who lived next door. At the same time, the children were developing plans for leaving home. Thus circumstances would soon force Clara to be mainly a wife instead of a daughter and mother. Did her complaint of "lack of communication" indicate that she had been thinking a lot about herself? What would be left for her when they moved away from her mother and the children were gone?

Why the Harrisons were coming to therapy was slowly being uncovered. They were facing one of the normal crises of any family development: the empty nest syndrome. But as always happens with alcoholic families, their problem was exacerbated by abnormal patterns developed over the years of disruptive alcoholic behavior. Ideally the forties and fifties are a time for adults to use their freedom to embark on new personal possiblities and to enrich the spouse subsystem, which is once again the basic family unit. Here Fred's drinking had put an immense distance between this couple. He had turned to AA and during the years of his recovery, Clara had become strongly involved with Al-Anon. As many Al-Anon members do, she had interpreted "independence" as overinvolvement with extrafamilial activities. So although she had learned to focus her psychological energy on constructive activity for herself, her role in the family was still largely what it had been during Fred's drinking years. Protected by the children and by their premature assumption of parental roles, she had become the outsider. But now, middle-aged, with her children leaving home, and not functioning fully as mother and spouse, Clara felt fundamentally threatened.

She spoke of feeling incompetent as a woman, wife, and mother. She wondered whether Fred was sexually attracted to the young men he was sponsoring in AA. Doubts about her own sexuality made her have doubts about Fred's. That took Fred entirely by surprise, and his response was reassurance with a great deal of tenderness. The exchange continued, and Clara shared with him a little more about her feelings and the need to reassess their relationship as husband and wife.

Slowly it was dawning on Clara that she was feeling incompetent as a woman and as such was unable to share a fulfilled sexual life with her husband. She began to talk about her self-image and the problems of separating from her mother and children. The resentments of the drinking years still smoldered, but an inkling of warmth in the relationship gave hope for rebuilding the marriage.

The main goal of therapy at this point was to help the couple open up to each other, start trusting, and work on developing the intimacy both wanted. Sessions were scheduled for this purpose, and many changes were accomplished as they both concentrated on learning to trust each other again. The therapist assigned several tasks. The couple were to meet for lunch several times a week and plan weekend trips away from the children. If they were going out to AA or Al-Anon meetings in the evenings, they were to leave the house together and return together. In therapy sessions they were encouraged to express their needs and to discuss what they wanted from each other. They were really surprised at how much they learned about each other in a short time.

When this was well under way, I suggested incorporating the children in the ongoing therapy. Fred and Clara understood the importance of this step and agreed to have them in a session. Because everybody in the family had a busy schedule, however, the therapist had to arrange to meet them on a Saturday morning.

Rosalie, Mary, and Freddie were good-looking young people, casually but carefully dressed. They showed some anxiety but were able to relax as the session started.

The therapist began by soliciting a picture of the family as they saw it. Mary picked up immediately, starting to describe a family with an actively drinking father. She said that Fred did not participate in family life, and that as a result, she and her sister and brother felt sorry for their mother and had to help and protect her.

The therapist pointed out that perhaps Mary was describing the family during Fred's drinking years and asked Mary whether this was the situation in the present. How did she see the family today? Mary immediately began to complain that her family exploited her. Over the years, she had taken on the housework. She was a neat and orderly person and worked hard to keep the house clean, while the others neither appreciated nor respected her.

As soon as Mary stopped, Freddie picked up and started to complain about Mary. He said that Mary continued to treat him like a child. For instance, when he left for a date, she would come to the door to inspect his dress, and he hated it.

Rosalie sat back, just listening to Mary and Freddie complain. She had been able to escape and to develop her life outside of the family, leaving Mary and Freddie to their overinvolved roles. Now just back from a trip to Europe, she was hunting for her own apartment and struggling to keep her two jobs.

After five years of sobriety, the children in this family were still functioning in the patterns developed during the drinking years. Mary was the substitute mother, and although she resented the role she had played all these years and felt hurt that no one appreciated her efforts, she had not yet relinquished her place. Freddie was still treated as the baby.

The therapist suggested that Clara discuss with Mary her

budding desire, expressed during a couple session, to take on more of a role within the family. Clara, still intimidated by her daughter, shook her head silently.

Freddie had been sitting in the background, seemingly an outsider. Still on the task of eliciting the family's picture of themselves in the present, the therapist asked Freddie how he was getting along with his father. Freddie replied briefly that no problems were evident but was interrupted by Clara's reminding him of what had happened during the years when Fred was drinking. At that time, Fred would promise his son they would go out on the boat on Saturday morning. They would get to the marina, Fred would go into the bar, and they would never cast off. "I didn't care," Freddie said. "After a while I got my own boat."

Was Clara using Freddie in this instance to express some of her own lingering resentments? Or was she assuming an old role?

Fred had sobered when Freddie was thirteen or fourteen, but he had made little attempt to get closer to his children, particularly his son. Now in the session, he gave it a try, saying he knew Freddie was having a difficult time trying to find a job. Fred indicated that he would like to help, but Freddie rejected him immediately. The silence was painful.

Suddenly Clara broke the impasse by putting herself on the hot seat, thus protecting both Fred and Freddie. Facing Mary, she said that she planned to take over the role of the woman of the house. Surprised, Mary challenged that, emphasizing her mother's lack of time due to overinvolvement with outside activities. Clara retorted that she and Fred had already discussed this and that she had decided to give up something, most probably her evening classes. This was significant; it showed that Clara had built up enough trust in Fred to use him as a support in front of the children. Mary could not immediately accept her mother's change — which would mandate a change in her own acquired pattern — and challenged again. Clara asked to be given a chance, and Fred nodded approval.

The family began to discuss practical matters, and everyone agreed to cooperate. Clara pointed out that her taking on more of the chores would give Mary the option of returning to school full-time—something Mary had been talking about for the past year. Mary looked up in surprise, and an expression of happiness crossed her face.

Since only one session would be held with this entire family, the therapist was forced to make some interpretations about the family organization. She questioned Rosalie, Mary, and Freddie, wondering whether they were still walking on eggs, protecting Fred, afraid that he might go back to his drinking. The three of them agreed. Fred picked this up immediately and told the children that this was his problem and that he was taking care of it, as he had for the past five years.

The therapist stated that the adopted protective patterns in the family, remaining through misunderstanding, were no longer appropriate and must be broken. Both parents and children had to recognize that the situation had changed and to act accordingly.

Freddie was in trouble. He resented his father but was not able to deal with him. The issues of father and son, barely touched on in this family, would require much work.

Mary must find something outside the family to fill her time and needs instead of continuing as a substitute mother. Rosalie was doing well, though some indications were evident that she was following her mother's pattern by overfilling her days.

These interpretations were made because the therapist sensed both strength and readiness for change in this family. In spite of the problems originally caused by alcoholism and now persisting in its wake, a lot of health was inherent in this family (a tribute to both Fred and Clara), which could be used to mobilize the family for change.

Couple sessions continued, focusing on developing intimacy. As the Harrisons became stronger and closer, they reported that Mary was much less involved with them. She did begin full-time school and gradually freed herself from household responsibilities. When the family moved to their new house, Mary got her own apartment.

Fred continued trying to reach his son. One day he called

the therapist, requesting to come for a session with his son. He said that Freddie was very upset because he still could not find a job but at the same time would not accept his father's help. It appeared that father and son could not talk to each other. This move by Fred to delineate a new subsystem in the family was an interesting additional proof that the Harrisons were continuing to seek change.

I arranged an early appointment. When they came to the session, Fred said immediately that they had been able to start talking and to share some ideas. The mere fact that he made the decision to call the therapist for help in communicating with Freddie strengthened his ability to open up the dialogue between them.

In the session, Fred explained to Freddie that although he did not want to impose his own values, he did want Freddie to know that he respected him as a young adult, and wanted to do whatever he could to make things easier for him while he was looking for work. This disclosure in turn helped Freddie ease up, and he managed to respond that although he had never felt close to his father, he understood that Fred was trying to help. He was willing to work on a relationship as long as his father understood that he had to do things his own way. He proceeded to expound on his plans. Fred pointed out ways he could help. It was agreed that they would work on handling things this way in the future and would call the therapist if they ran into problems.

In spite of Fred's sustained sobriety, the Harrison family had remained trapped in their old patterns, with both Fred and Clara working on their individual development without integrating their changes into a family structure. As a result, a stalemate developed over the years that was hampering the children's growth and was undercutting a source of support for both spouses. Once the barriers erected by all members of the family started to be removed in therapy, the family began to create the missing links and to build up the existing ones.

The Harrisons' case is a good example of two basic therapeutic principles. First, it is often advisable to bring about changes in the family by first attempting to rebuild the spouses' relationship. Assuming the couple is willing and ready, they can be helped in pulling together into a team. When work with the children begins, a foundation for change has already been established. Second, family members of any age may have to learn that complementarity does not conflict with autonomy. For Clara, autonomy had meant being an outsider. She had to learn that she could relate to Fred as a wife without sacrificing her sense of self. Freddie, at a very difficult age, had to learn that living his own life did not preclude his need to develop a relationship with a father he had never really known.

9

Working with Shame and Stigma: *The Clatworthys*

"Ghetto alcoholism" is often more than alcoholism. It is all the problems of alcoholism combined with the stress of poverty and/or discrimination. A low-income family does not have the safety margin that often helps better-off families cope with alcoholism. There are no seminars on alcoholism and the executive, no company health insurance plans. Friends and relatives may lack the resources to help as they would like. Furthermore, to a striving, lower-middle-class black family like the Clatworthys, to whom moving up was almost a religion, alcoholism can carry a double stigma. Not only is it a personal "weakness" but it is also a threat to the children's future.

The Clatworthys were referred to me by a job supervisor, who said that Mrs. Clatworthy, age thirty-five, was potentially one of his best workers. But over the past year and a half she had been failing in job performance. He had suggested that she call a doctor, but she had explained that the problem was not her health but her worry over her two sons. They were playing hooky and no longer working up to capacity in school. She had taken Daniel, age sixteen, to a child guidance clinic at the school's suggestion, but nothing had happened and she was very discouraged. She did not know what else to do.

The job supervisor told me that the Clatworthys were an upwardly mobile black family, highly invested in escaping from the cycle of limited education and limited opportunity. Jean, who worked as a file clerk, was determined to see all her children through school and to live what she called "a decent life." This was an uphill struggle, the supervisor said, and the family had had to move to cheaper apartments several times. But the drive remained. The supervisor expressed concern because Mrs. Clatworthy's job was the only chance she and her children had to break the poverty cycle.

The supervisor mentioned one more thing—something he said he doubted even the children knew. Mr. Clatworthy had been an alcoholic. After many years of increasing alcohol abuse, he had developed cirrhosis of the liver. One day he collapsed and died in the street. Within days, Jean had moved, with Daniel, then age nine, Steven, age eight, and Linette, age four. Mandy was born four months later. The move took the family away from the support of a concerned extended family and community network. But Jean Clatworthy had to get far away from anyone who knew her shame: an alcoholic husband and father.

A similar reaction is expressed in Betty Smith's *A Tree Grows in Brooklyn:*

> The doctor asked necessary questions: the full name and place of birth and date of birth and so on. Finally Katie asked him a question.
> "What are you writing down there—what he died from, I mean."
> "Acute alcoholism and pneumonia."
> . . . "I don't want you to write down," said Katie slowly and steadily, "that he died from drinking too much. Write that he died of pneumonia alone."
> "Madam, I have to state the entire truth." . . .
> "Look," said Kate. "I got two nice children. They're going to grow up to amount to something. It isn't their fault that their father . . . that he died from what you said. It would mean a lot to me if I could tell them that their father died of pneumonia alone."

The supervisor suggested that Jean bring the children to me with the purpose of making an assessment of the family. Jean agreed, and an appointment was made.

After a few cancelled appointments, Jean appeared with her four children. The children were well groomed but cautious and reserved. When they entered the room, they sat in a circle. Jean looked shy and withdrawn, as contrasted with the children's cautious appraisal of the therapist. She chose a seat outside the circle. Invited to join the group, she did so but without changing expression.

Jean started to list the family problems. She focused immediately on her difficulties, dealing with her two sons, particularly Daniel, now age sixteen. Lately he had become more disobedient and defiant. He insisted on going back to the old neighborhood on weekends in spite of her disapproval. Jean added that she had been a widow for six years and found it difficult to manage the children, the household chores, and a job.

Daniel reacted angrily. He said that he could not understand why they had to come to "this place" to discuss "family affairs" they could take care of at home. But Jean reemphasized her need to get help. She felt progressively more and more unable to do everything alone. She recognized that the children were trying to help her, especially the girls and Steven, whom she described as a "good boy." But that was not enough.

The therapist picked up on Daniel's anger at being at the agency and asked Jean whether she had explained to the children why they were coming here. Jean said that she had "just told them that they had to come." This gave the therapist an opportunity to involve the children in the therapeutic process by questioning each of them. Were they aware of the problems their mother had just mentioned? She met with silence. No one volunteered information, so the therapist tried to draw out each child in turn, going around the circle. Sensing the children's wariness, she proceeded gently, working her way cautiously around.

Steven ignored the question and barely indicated that he had heard. Linette echoed her mother: the family problems were the boys' disobedience and fighting. When Daniel's turn came, he pinpointed himself as the problem, the troublemaker, and again expressed annoyance at being there. He repeated that he could not see any reason for coming. When I spoke to Mandy she smiled, looking at her mother and sister. Daniel immediately interrupted, saying, "She doesn't know; leave her alone!"

At this point, Steven also spoke like his mother, focusing on the fighting, but said that they had no real problem.

The family members were very tense, controlling their emotions. Steven was sitting very quietly and rigidly, holding on to his hat and staring at the floor. Daniel was still defiant and protective of the others. They all appeared confused and unsure of how they should answer. It was hard to tell whether they were defying their mother or protecting her and whether this reflected their behavior at home.

Mrs. Clatworthy insisted again that the main problem was disciplining the children. She could not do it alone. "They would have listened to their father," she said, but they would not mind her.

Since the father had been mentioned, the therapist asked about him. The response was silence, and then Mrs. Clatworthy said briefly that he had died quite suddenly before Mandy was born.

Daniel interrupted saying that the father was the problem. It seemed the "ghost" in the family was surfacing. The therapist tried again to focus on the father's death, and again she met with silence. Did they ever speak of him, or mourn his loss? Was he ever mentioned in the family?

A family secret is symptomatic of a family's problems. Jean's life was dominated by the specter of alcoholism. It was not only a threat in itself but also a symbol of everything she was trying to escape. As a result, the father's alcoholism was strongly influencing the way she saw her children.

Jean changed the subject abruptly, explaining that the move after her husband's death had taken her children away from her family and from their old neighborhood. She could not afford the rents in that area, so she had had to take what she could get. The children had had to change schools, and it was difficult to get back to see her family.

Daniel complained that he was forbidden to spend Sundays with Grandmother and visit friends in the old neighborhood. His mother thought he was going out to drink and smoke pot. But he was not. He just liked to see his family. Steven added that he liked to visit too. He was very close to one of his uncles, and that was the only chance he had to see him.

It seemed that Jean's mother had taken care of the children even before Mr. Clatworthy's death. The therapist asked herself whether Jean's move had put her in the position of having to learn to be a mother as well as a single parent. Had the children experienced not only the loss of a father but also the loss of their primary caretaker?

In order to set some working goals, the therapist asked the family members what they would like to change. Again silence fell; the only one who replied was Linette, who said the furniture was in poor condition and that the linoleum needed replacing. This was again corrected by Daniel, who seemed very protective of the image of his family.

By the end of the session, the therapist felt that little had been accomplished. The strongest impression was derived from the impact of the father's death in the family function. She thought that mourning for the father would be important for the Clatworthys, especially if Jean and the older children could bring up some of the good things they remembered. By talking about the father, they might also come to understand that he was a sick person and not just a drunkard of whom they must be ashamed. Perhaps Jean could learn to detach from the shame that had been such an influence on her life.

None of this was expressed to the family, but Jean may well have picked up the impression that Mr. Clatworthy would have to be discussed. Although she agreed to come back for a few more sessions, the family never returned.

After several appointments had been broken, rescheduled, and broken again, the therapist reached out, telephoning Jean. Jean said frankly that she felt Mr. Clatworthy's death would have to be discussed in family sessions and that she did not want that to happen. Daniel, the oldest, remembered his father's drinking, but the others, the girls, "didn't know." She wanted them to have the image of a good father, not a drunkard. Some of her anger against her husband showed for the first time in this conversation, but when the therapist again suggested that they set another appointment, Jean refused firmly. She simply would not take the risk of opening this area for the children and herself.

A therapeutic contract might have been made to continue

without talking about the father. But this would have been extremely difficult, and probably Jean could never have trusted the therapist to keep away from this area.

Furthermore, concentrating on Jean's difficulties might have raised the prospect of losing her job, because Jean knew that her job supervisor knew me. Focusing on changes would have been difficult if not impossible. Under the circumstances, I accepted Jean's decision.

Jean Clatworthy's life was one long flight from alcoholism. The dreadful secret had impelled her to move away from the extended family, which could have been her support. In trying to prove herself the mother she felt society expected her to be, she was failing to recognize the needs of her growing children. Her great fear of drinking, as well as of pot, blinded her to their adolescent search for independence. She was trying to keep them home and safe, and her very concern was driving them to escape.

Much could have been done to help the Clatworthys through Al-Anon, Alateen, alcoholism education, and helping Jean and the boys learn how to negotiate in a manner more appropriate to a mother and her teenage children. But unless some crisis brought Jean back to therapy, her decision would have to stand.

Denial was part of Jean Clatworthy's life even after her husband's death. The illusion that the children did not know about their father's drinking continued and would not change unless she faced the reality of the cause of his death.

Shame, fear, and the stigma of alcoholism played an important role in this family. To cover up for her husband's death from alcoholism, Jean took the children away from the neighborhood where they had grown up and where she had a network of support that could have created a more nurturing environment for the children and herself. Her job performance will probably continue to deteriorate, and only if overwhelmed by some future crisis will she return to treatment.

10

~~~~~~~~~~~~

Options in Reuniting
a Family:
The Collinses

Some alcoholism programs have developed longer term (thirty to ninety days) inpatient rehabilitation units for those in need of a temporary sheltered environment after detoxification. The populations served by these programs come mostly from the very deteriorated victims of long years of drinking. Some patients, however, have no home to return to, and the halfway house becomes their next step. The main modality of treatment is group therapy, with reinforced life learning experiences. From this background, the individual may start to reenter community life. Specific programs attempt a further step — namely, a return to the family of origin. The latter approach may create differences of opinion among therapists.

John Collins was admitted to an alcoholism rehabilitation unit at the request of his sisters, Mary and Cathleen. Their information was that John, age sixty-five, had been drinking all his life. He had been hospitalized for alcoholism several times but never followed treatment recommendations after discharge. More than ever, the sisters were concerned because John, now in very poor health, was facing mandatory retirement. In the intervening years, he had isolated himself from the family and had no home to go to. He also was becoming more violent during drinking sprees, and if he came to live with them, he might become dangerous.

John was admitted to the unit, but before the alcoholism counselor had the first session with the patient, she was bombarded by phone calls from both sisters. They were full of questions and advice and called repeatedly to find out whether John had exploded and perhaps had become violent.

99

The counselor met with John and returned very confused. Prepared by the sisters to take precautions against a possibly violent man, she found herself talking to a submissive, withdrawn individual ready to do anything the counselor suggested.

John offered the following information. He was the oldest of five siblings and the only one who never married. His father had died when they were all very young, and John left home shortly afterward. For a while, he drifted across the country and finally landed a job as a deckhand on an ore freighter. He had remained with the company ever since, working his way up to first mate. "And I'm the best damn mate in the service," he growled. The counselor encouraged him to talk about his job and discovered that John was extremely bitter about the "fool rule" that was going to force him into retirement in a few months. John was adamant; he was going to fight that with everything he had. He would get the union to back him and force the company to keep him on.

As the meeting unfolded, the counselor began to realize that John actually knew he could not retain his job. But he simply could not envision any alternative to the life he had led for forty years. He was started on individual therapy, made some progress, and began to think more realistically about his future. At that point, the counselor suggested having a few sessions with the participation of his sisters. John agreed submissively, and I was called in as a consultant in family therapy. Both sisters were anxious to come, and a meeting was arranged.

As soon as we met Mary, the youngest of the siblings, we recognized a family powerhouse. An officer in the Salvation Army, Mary radiated righteous authority. Her sister, Cathleen, was small and thin, fragile and doll-like. John greeted them politely and then sat down to stare at the floor.

Mary described John in no uncertain terms as the family's lost sheep. He had been a drinker all his life and squandered his money. Cathleen, with tears in her eyes, expressed a desire only to see her big brother improve and get closer to the family. Ever since their father's death she had hoped that John, her eldest brother, would take the father's place in the family. But he never had. He had failed them all. Mary agreed that his job was the cause for his lost contact with the family. He had spent most of his life traveling, and when he did come for visits, he stayed in a hotel and spent his vacation drinking. Now he had no place to go.

John sat in the corner like a little boy being scolded by a parent, occasionally looking to Cathleen for support. The therapist tried to draw him out a little and to talk about his retirement. John growled that this was unfair. The company was pushing him out after nearly forty years of hard work. He appreciated his sisters' desire to help, but his problem was forced retirement. He had always been a traveling man. What was he supposed to do now? Mary interjected that drinking was not a solution. At that point, silence fell. It was clear that Mary and John put emphasis on different issues.

John was trying to prove that he was not a bum. Mary repeated that she wanted to help John, but not to go back home to live with them. He must find a place of his own to settle. The message was clear: we want you, but we do not want to take care of you. John found his sisters' behavior very confusing. Their welcome was forgiving but conditional. Though he never mentioned an interest in going back to live with them, they made it clear that this would not be acceptable.

Easter was approaching, and both sisters were anxious to have John spend it with the family. They talked about how much his nieces and nephews were looking forward to meeting him again. It was their belief that the holiday spirit would make his visit much easier.

Toward the end of the session, the tension had eased. Before they left, Mary took some money from her purse and offered it to John. Asked why she was giving John money, she explained that she collected his paychecks, banked them for him, and gave him cash as he needed it. Suddenly it became apparent that he had maintained contact with the family. John accepted the money but studied his sister's face to see whether he was to be scolded for irresponsibility once again. Both women began to cry. Here was an older brother, they said, unable to function on his own. John did not try to defend himself. He seemed to be used to these scenes.

In a subsequent session, we learned that John had gone to Easter Sunday dinner with the family. But unknown to the sisters, he had invited another man from the rehabilitation unit to accompany him. John admitted in the session that he did not feel strong enough to face the family alone. He had hoped that the presence of a stranger would keep the family from talking about his problems. This session became a repetition of the first, with both women saying again and again how much the family wanted to help John. The counselor pointed out, however, that on the one hand, they were treating John as an incompetent man, and that on the other, they were urging him to become head of the family. If John was to take charge of his life, their attitude must change. Helped by this interpretation, John began to "open up" and to share some of his own doubts about the future. He did not feel strong enough, however, to make promises about specific changes. In the meantime, he continued in individual and group therapy. His self-esteem was growing. He actively participated in the rehab unit's daily activities, in which he proved to himself that he could socialize without drinking.

Because plans for discharge had to be arranged, the counselor decided to present John's case at a staff meeting. The discussion centered around the treatment John should be offered. The question divided the staff. Assuming he would remain sober, should we leave him to continue a free, unattached life on discharge? Or should we try to encourage closeness to his family until he developed his own social network? The conflict was never resolved. At discharge, the counselor arranged for John to go to a halfway house and never learned the outcome.

The ideal approach in John's case would have been to use the family and AA as basic support. Family therapy, however, would not have meant returning John to live with his sisters in the role of a father figure. Individual therapy would be added to help him chart an independent pursuit of personal wishes.

When working with elderly alcoholics, it is important to assess the onset of the heavy drinking. In John's case, he had drunk in his early years, and in the process of getting to an advanced stage of alcoholism, he had disconnected himself from his family.

Mental health professionals sometimes misconceive of family therapy as a method that forces people to reattach to their families of origin. In John's case, this misconception blocked an approach that could have allowed him to be part of his family of origin as an individual and to strengthen his personal development. It might also have been possible to help him connect with a network of support to supplement or replace the family of origin (Zimberg and others, 1985).

11

~~~~~~~~~~

When the Alcoholic
Is Unreachable:
The McCarthys

Therapy of an alcoholic family should always include the alcoholic member, and abuse of alcohol should be one of the therapeutic targets. Unfortunately, making such a contract is not always possible. In some cases, the alcoholic proves genuinely unreachable. In others, he simply refuses to commit himself to therapy. When this happens, we must still attempt to free the other family members from the effects alcoholism has on their lives. A change in the life of the family members will usually, in some measure, reach the alcoholic.

The McCarthys were living the comfortable life of the midwestern small-town upper-middle class when Richard's company transferred them to New York City. Lisa was extremely reluctant to leave her family and childhood friends, but the couple agreed that Lisa would make plans to go back to Nebraska whenever she felt too lonely in New York.

Lisa had been a devoted wife and mother but also close to her own family. Now the children were grown and out of the home. Richard Jr., age twenty-four, and Jim, age twenty-two, were married. Mary Ann, age twenty, was away at college. Richard's job had always required a lot of traveling, which Lisa had never minded as long as she had her own family close by. Now she found herself on her own in a strange city. She seemed to lack the resources to come to terms with these changes in her life, and for the first time, she was confronted with the fact that she had not recognized up to now: Richard was a "problem drinker."

Lisa began to lose weight and developed some digestive

problems. Very concerned about her health, she consulted a doctor and volunteered some concern about emotional discomforts. She was depressed and very anxious, especially at night. Her husband often came home late, she said, and she suddenly found herself talking about her husband: how Richard was prolonging the "happy hour" until nine or ten at night; how he often just made it to his easy chair before falling asleep, unable to talk to her or to join her in eating the dinners she carefully kept warm. As the doctor questioned her gently, she found herself confiding how one night she had come home to find Richard unconscious on the floor. She could not even get him to come to the phone to talk to the children these days. He was almost always "asleep."

Lisa was lucky. The doctor she had picked knew something about alcoholism and, more importantly, believed that wives of alcoholics can be helped. So instead of reaching for his prescription pad, he firmly instructed Lisa to get in touch with Al-Anon.

This upset Lisa badly, but she decided to attend a few Al-Anon meetings and find out what this was about. The first meeting frightened her, but she found the factual information very useful. She began to understand the fact that Richard was an alcoholic and to learn how other women were facing similar situations. Lisa decided to continue with Al-Alon. She also made an appointment to see me.

At this point, Lisa was underweight and shy, still terrified after eight months in the big city. She traveled only by bus, a recognizable thing from "home," and refused to enter the subway. She presented herself as a highly incompetent woman, lost without the guidance of her family.

She was in great need of support, but the only people in New York she could resort to were her husband's colleagues and their wives. That frightened her because any discussion of her situation would reveal Richard's drinking problem and might jeopardize his job. Unable as yet to trust the Al-Anon group, she pleaded for help, anxious to try anything to feel better.

We agreed that Lisa would start individual therapy. I told her that at some point it would be necessary to involve Richard.

Lisa said that he would never agree and preferred to focus on making herself more competent.

The therapist's goal at this point was to help Lisa concentrate on aspects of her life apart from Richard's drinking, build up her strength and capabilities, and develop her own interests and life goals, as was appropriate for any woman her age. In this way, I hoped Lisa could reduce her worry about Richard's drinking and get off his back. An improvement in Lisa could be a way of changing Richard and possibly of reaching out to get him to explore the possibility of therapy.

Lisa began to improve rapidly as her strength and competence developed under therapy. Soon she found a job, which she enjoyed. She insisted, however, on working part-time so that she would have the opportunity of visiting her family back in Nebraska. Although she had kept in close touch with her children by phone, the opportunity to visit her sons and the rest of her family contributed substantially to her well-being. Each time she came back, she had more energy to face the situation. The city appeared less threatening, and the Al-Anon group became a strong network of support. She began to take some courses in pottery—which had long been an interest of hers—and gradually built her skills into a successful small business.

Suddenly a crisis appeared. Mary Ann dropped out of college and was coming home. Lisa did not know how she could cope with her daughter and was frightened that Mary Ann would find out about Richard's drinking. The therapist encouraged Lisa to stop covering up for Richard. She was to talk frankly to Mary Ann, explain about her father's illness, and steer the daughter to deal with her directly. Lisa did so. She also invited Mary Ann to come to a session with the therapist, but her daughter declined. Lisa handled this problem successfully on her own.

Overall a new pattern developed in the spouse unit of this family. Lisa detached herself from her husband's drinking but not from Richard as a husband. With no intention of separating, she simply accepted his illness. They went to church together and had an active social life. When Richard had too much to drink, Lisa would insist they leave the car and take a cab home. When he drank excessively, she would leave him alone, but she made sure that his meals were prepared. When he passed out at dinner or other times and she had to leave the house to go to a meeting or a class, she made sure that no cigarettes were left burning and that he was comfortably perched but did not let his behavior interfere with her own plans.

The therapist urged Lisa to invite Richard to join in their sessions. According to Lisa, he simply refused. Apparently Richard understood that he was an alcoholic, but he saw no reason to stop drinking. It was not interfering with his job, and he had no sense that he was neglecting his family. Lisa accepted his denial. She decided to continue working on herself and building up her own life, freeing Richard to do as he pleased.

Lisa did take several of the steps I suggested to make sure Richard stayed in contact with his children. She made a point of calling their sons whenever Richard was available to talk with them. Mary Ann had settled in an artist's colony in Chicago, and she also kept in close contact by phone, particularly whenever she needed money. Lisa always referred Mary Ann to her father. In the past, she had probably acted as a go-between for her husband and children. Now she carefully began to remove herself from that role so that Richard would have a stronger sense of playing a needed role within his family.

Through individual therapy, Lisa McCarthy built up a life for herself that included a dysfunctioning husband. She accepted the problems as something that would continue, just as she accepted alcoholism as a chronic illness from which Richard would suffer for the foreseeable future. Not only did she teach herself to see Richard as a sick person and to accept that without resentment, but she also helped the children and the extended family see him in the same way. She was functioning well and so was her family, and Lisa was satisfied with that.

How would this case be evaluated therapeutically? From Lisa's point of view, therapy was successful. Personal gratification through new interests and maintaining a well-functioning family were sufficient to compensate for the stresses of living with an active alcoholic.

The ideal of a recovered alcoholic living happily within a changed family system cannot always be achieved. In the

McCarthy case, the failure to reach Richard did not change the fact that Lisa's functioning improved greatly through therapy, as did the functioning of the family network. Lisa's acceptance of alcoholism as a chronic illness made it possible for her to detach from her husband's drinking problem and to develop a new life for herself without separating from him. In this case, an intervention to reach her husband for treatment might have been possible, but since Lisa was not ready for it, her wishes were respected.

Lisa keeps in touch with the therapist, sending Christmas cards that always include a short note. Last year she mentioned that her husband had had to stop drinking due to serious problems with his liver. Only time will tell what that may mean to this couple.

12

~~~~~~~~~~~~~~

When Progress
Is Uneven:
The Stewarts

*Failure in work performance is often an important factor in motivating
an alcoholic toward treatment. This was true for Peter Stewart, who committed himself to the AA program, sobered, and maintained his recovery.
But when the family functioning does not improve, due to another member's alcoholism, there will still be adverse effects.*

Both parents in the Stewart family were alcoholics and
had been since their teens. Peter was a factory maintenance
worker; Emily was a housewife; they had two children.

In his early thirties, Peter Stewart hit a particularly bad
period, and for the first time, his drinking began to affect his
job performance seriously. Increasing absenteeism and poor performance at work caused his supervisor to refer him to the factory's employee health services. The counselor there confronted
Peter with his heavy drinking, suggested that he be detoxified,
and put him in touch with AA. Peter followed through with these
suggestions. He committed himself to the AA program. His
drinking stopped, and he began to recover. His job performance
also improved. He felt, however, that his wife's alcoholism threatened his recovery, and so he left the household. He could see
his life changing, and he was delighted. The counseling service
closed the case; prognosis: promising.

But an important area of Peter's life remained unchanged:
his family life. Eight months after his first referral, he called
the counselor again. This time his concern was for Emily, still
an active alcoholic, and his children, particularly his son, Marty,
age twelve, who had been involved in some minor delinquency
"because of the influence of bad friends."

Employee counseling services are designed to focus on helping the individual and on improving the individual's work performance. But Peter Stewart's counselor realized that the functioning of the individual on the job and elsewhere cannot help but be affected when his or her family is in difficulty. He referred Peter to a family therapist.

The family therapist's first contact with Mr. Stewart was by phone. The case record stated that he had been working on his drinking and that his current concern was for his wife and son. Peter explained that his wife, Emily, had been trying to sober up through AA and other services since her husband had stopped drinking but had not succeeded.

Knowing that Mrs. Stewart was drinking but not knowing how intoxicated she might be, the therapist then made plans to see the couple without the two children.

When the couple came to the session, Emily had just attained three days of sobriety. She was pleased to be sober, but her appearance showed long-term neglect. Her hair was dyed blond, but it had not been done for so long that it was a combination of blond and brown. Her face was red and swollen. Her eyes were bloodshot, and she was hiding her body with her arms and a too-tight jacket, which she refused to take off. Peter, in contrast, was nicely dressed in a short-sleeved shirt and a neat pair of slacks. He looked so well that, even though he was also in his late thirties, he looked ten years younger than his wife.

The couple did not meet each other's eyes. It was very difficult for them to face each other or the therapist. But they were there with a common concern — their children — and Peter's concern for another human being suffering from alcoholism.

The couple session focused on Emily and how she would handle her drinking problem. The therapist assured them that Marty's problems would also be a focus during therapy. But alcoholism was such a core problem in this family that nothing could be achieved until this had been dealt with. The plan initially was to help Emily deal on an individual basis with her drinking. Peter could not help her because his own sobriety was still threatened. They could easily have fallen back into the old pattern of this family system, with Peter acting as husband and father — but also as drinking partner.

Emily explained that she had committed herself to the AA ninety-day program. Peter was very supportive of her efforts, and he promised to drive her to AA meetings. They talked about the children, and Peter said again that he was concerned about Marty. Marty had been unjustly blamed for the theft of a bike. He was a very shy and nonaggressive child who could not defend himself. The couple was reassured that a session including the children was planned for the following week, but since it was obvious that Emily's mind was not entirely clear, any further exploration of issues in this session was inadvisable. The therapist told Emily to keep in touch with her by phone. A time was arranged for Emily to call the therapist each day to report on her doings. This is a therapeutic technique that supports the AA philosophy of staying sober one day at a time. During the week, Emily called the therapist faithfully. She felt encouraged and supported, and she was looking forward to coming to the next session with the children.

Emily succeeded in maintaining sobriety. The therapist knew this, but she was amazed at the changes already apparent at the next session. Emily was nicely dressed, her face had returned to normal, and her mind was clear. It was obvious that Emily was already anxious to be seen in her recovering state — an excellent sign of progess.

Tina, age eight, was dressed like a fifteen-year-old, in high heels and panty hose. Her behavior, too, was that of a little lady. She smiled all the time. Marty, like his father, was very much dressed up for this session, but he seemed more his age. Both children were very shy.

When we started to discuss family problems, Marty at the beginning was mute. Tina, with some prompting, admitted that the family had some problems; then she smiled again, and she could not really say what they were. The closest she could come was to talk about their house, neglected now because her father was not there. Things were breaking down, and no one was around to fix them. She looked at her father but said no more.

Emily, too, had difficulty describing her needs. She admitted to little trouble and that both children were doing well. The therapist allowed silence to fall. Then Emily admitted that

Marty was not doing so well in school. He would like his father to help him, she said, but his father was not there. Because she was not as well educated as her husband, she could not help Marty with his homework.

Marty remained quiet. The therapist tried to reach him by chatting about his interests. Marty said that he did not participate in after-school activities. He had to come straight home, pick up his bike, do the shopping, and then come back to help his mother. The therapist asked about supper. Both children smiled and said that was no problem; they both knew how to do hamburgers and frozen fries.

A picture of the family began to develop. Peter, understandably concerned about the effects his wife's drinking might have on his own sobriety, had been avoiding the house. Emily's drinking had worsened. As a result, the children had been neglected and badly affected by their parents' problems. Both of them were taking on adult roles in order to help their mother, and Tina showed the pseudomaturity often seen in alcoholics' children. Though Marty longed to join the adolescent peer group, he was so desperate for friends that he allowed himself to be the scapegoat of the neighborhood toughs. He was also experimenting with pot.

It was important at this point to give this family the sense that they were working for change. The therapist suggested continuing with couple sessions, in which Peter and Emily could work on functioning as a parental team. Combined with these would be sessions including the children, which would focus on actual parental issues. The therapist would also continue seeing Emily individually, to support her individual needs. Close contact by phone would continue; Emily would need a lot of support to build up her sobriety. The family agreed.

Another goal, yet to be discussed with the family, was to work with Peter and Emily as spouses. In this strategy, the therapist was following Minuchin's paradigm (1974) of the family as a system differentiated into spouse and parental subsystems. Peter and Emily were concerned parents, anxious to help their children. But they both had been alcoholics for the entire twelve years of their married life. All the tasks of spouse subsystem formation had been handicapped and probably overshadowed by drinking. If any problem existed in their sexual relationship, it would have been ascribed to drinking. Learning how to read each other and support each other had obviously been impossible. Patterns for negotiating and resolving conflict had not developed. If Peter and Emily were to build a relationship as spouses — and their ability to do this remained to be seen — they would have to start from scratch.

After a few sessions, the Stewarts began to get in touch with their needs and expectations of each other. Emily was afraid of saying too much. She was still unsure of her sobriety, and she would not express her needs or what she wanted from her husband. But after she had celebrated her ninety days of sobriety in AA, she began to feel stronger. She started to talk about her needs. She definitely wanted Peter to take over some parental tasks — the children needed their father. But it was obvious that she felt considerable ambivalence about having him back in the house. She simply did not know how to relate to this man as a husband in a relationship that did not include drinking. Furthermore, the Stewarts had been separated for almost a year, and during that year, they had had little contact. Emily felt confused and unsure about the role of wife, and it was obvious that much work in this area would be necessary.

When summer came, the family began to talk about a vacation. The therapist seized on this as an opportunity for expanding the family experience. Emily had been taking over more and more of the household chores. Both Marty and Tina, though pleased at her increasing competence, sensed an empty space in their lives, left by giving up the responsibilities they had carried. They both needed to develop age-appropriate interests. Marty in particular was still far too shy, coming to life only when he discussed his hobby: geography. The therapist arranged summer camp for the children. They were also referred to Alateen.

Both Peter and Emily were doing very well in their recovery, and slowly Peter was growing closer to his family. They planned a family weekend at the beach and carried it through successfully. The children were delighted.

During the summer, the apartment Peter was sharing with

another man had to be given up. The couple agreed that he should move back home, but this presented great problems for them both. The therapist worked with them intensively, helping Peter reenter the household and family and helping the couple deal together with the children on a day-to-day basis. Peter began to work on the falling plaster and broken linoleum, and slowly the couple began to work together on other tasks. They could no longer use drinking as the escape from and excuse for all problems, but they were willing to face the difficulties of building a relationship as husband and wife.

The favorable prognosis for the Stewart family is based partly on the strengths inherent in this family, particularly the parents' determination to help their children before early signs of difficulty worsen. Their ability to keep themselves sober and to remain closely involved with AA also gives hope that changes can be accomplished.

In the Stewart family, both parents were alcoholic. The recovery of Peter, the husband and father, did not improve the functioning of the family, and his performance at work remained unsatisfactory. Emily's drinking increased, and as a consequence, her children assumed charge not only of themselves but also of Emily, since Peter had left the household for fear of starting to drink again.

The intervention of the employee assistance program, due to concerns with his work, brought Emily into treatment and made her look at her drinking problem. Daily contact with the therapist motivated her to start recovery and, through family sessions, slowly to look into her relationship with her husband. With drinking out of the picture, the spouse subsystem began to develop again, and at the same time, they began to learn the roles of parents.

Part 3

Women,
Family Therapy,
and Alcoholism

13

Five Women Affected by Alcoholism

Alcoholism is a disease classically focused on the individual male alcoholic, shutting out the "other victims" of alcoholism. Now we are beginning to recognize the wives and daughters of alcoholics as a large population who may have suffered every degree of mental and physical cruelty. Perhaps worse, they are trapped in interactional patterns that confine them to the role of "alcoholic's wife" — that is, "enabler," "codependent."

This chapter describes a group of women I met through individual, couple, family, and/or group therapy. Four of them had married alcoholics. The fifth was unable to separate sufficiently from her alcoholic family of origin to establish a life of her own. All were depressed and angry, and characteristically these women had difficulty seeing themselves as individuals — people in their own right, with their own needs and goals. They seemed to have no role in life other than being victims of alcoholism. Even in therapy, their individual needs and desires had been subordinate to the needs of the alcoholic. They were seeking therapy to find support in bearing their pain, not to free themselves as individuals.

The married women in this group were in their thirties and forties. All of them were well educated and doing well in their careers. Not one was alcoholic. Most of them, as is not uncommon among wives of alcoholics, were overweight. All of them had conflicts with their sexuality, and several presented homosexual fears. All of them were highly skeptical about the possibility of establishing healthy relationships with men and thought they lacked the attributes necessary for good experiences as women. Intensely aware that they had gotten themselves into relationships with alcoholics, they were terrified of repeating the same mistakes in forming future relationships.

These women had another factor in common that promptly came to the front in therapy. They all were still closely involved with their families of origin, and, interestingly enough, four of them had alcoholic parents.

Although statistics have never been gathered, a growing body of anecdotal material suggests that this syndrome is not uncommon: wives of alcoholics, like alcoholics themselves, tend to come from families affected by alcoholism. In the case of the alcoholics themselves, this may be partly hereditary. But why should their wives, who may often refuse to drink, have entered into union with them? We are beginning to learn how traumatic the effects of parental alcoholism can be for children, particularly in regard to their development of sex and role identity. It may be that the daughters of alcoholics grow up in an environment so skewed that they never appreciate that other options are open to them. They learn to live primarily as adjuncts to alcoholism. And this is the life they establish for themselves in their marriages.

The Group

This group was formed out of the planned ending of an earlier women's group. The members of the first group were women in their fifties and sixties. One was married to an active alcoholic, another to an intermittent alcoholic, and another to a man who had stopped drinking but had begun abusing other drugs. In late middle age, these women were not set to effect many changes in their lives beyond finding ways to accommodate to the reality of coping with their husbands' addiction.

When Irene, a woman of thirty-seven, came to the therapist for marital therapy, the therapist suggested that she join this women's group. Irene became a group member, though very passive and quiet, for a short time. When the group agreed to stop meeting, Irene wanted to continue. The therapist was in the process of beginning a group with younger women. Irene joined this, and, as the "old-timer," she quickly became the group leader.

But the therapeutic focus for this second group was different. These younger women wanted to create lives of their own. If they could manage within their marriages, they would, but if not, they would go it alone. Group rules were different from the former group. Support was combined with confrontation—a new experience for the group members who were involved with Al-Anon.

Wives of alcoholics have a great need of support, and in group situations, they tend to provide this support to each other by protecting, denying, and/or cheering up. As a result, such a group can sometimes become unhealthy—comforting but static. Some Al-Anon members learn a pattern of immediate gratification: when you feel pain, you are to call another member, tell her about it, and she will comfort you. When these patterns began to emerge in this group, the therapist firmly confronted these tendencies and steered the women to acknowledge their problems and to work them through. They were to look closely into what aspects of their lives were worth change. Furthermore, they were not encouraged to keep in touch outside of the group context. If a crisis came up, they were to call the therapist, with the option of sharing their experiences with the group later on, if they wished. Pain was alleviated in the group but not with the immediate comfort that becomes an end in itself.

The results of this orientation were positive. These women had to learn to know themselves as people. The overriding themes in the group were anger, depression, and self-worth. Eventually they all became very open, giving warmth and support, and were able to experience the closeness they needed in the group. But for a long time they had difficulty confronting each other in the attempt to deal with core issues—their anger, their sexuality, and what they would do to make their lives better.

Irene

When Irene came to the therapist for marriage counseling, she was thirty-seven, of medium height, quite thin, with hair strag-

gling to her shoulders, making her small face look like a carica-
ture of a mannequin. She had had individual therapy before,
so she immediately began to report the details she assumed the
therapist wanted. Her mother had died of alcoholism, and her
father had committed suicide shortly afterward. She had a married sister, seven years younger, with whom she kept in sporadic
contact. She never heard anymore from her brother. A native
of Nova Scotia, she had left her family in her early twenties to
come to New York to study art, but an accident had injured
the nerves in her right hand, and she had had to give up paint-
ing. She worked now as an administrative assistant and considered herself very competent in her job.

Irene cried when she talked about her parents' deaths, but
she also assured the therapist that she had already mourned
them. What she wanted now was help with her marriage.

Irene said that her husband was an Ivy League graduate, "very intellectual" but in an advanced stage of alcoholism.
He would sober up, get a job, and maintain both for two to
three weeks. Then he would begin drinking again. She had gone
to some Al-Anon meetings, but she did not like the group of
women there. She recognized their anger and their inability to
face it or work on it, which she found extremely depressing.

The therapist saw Irene and her husband. He was a "nice
guy" type, very intellectual, as she had said, but tight-lipped
and divorced from his feelings. The only way Irene could arouse
any reaction from him was by yelling and screaming. He would
make no commitment to work on his drinking or to go to AA,
so the therapist decided to see Irene on an individual basis and
also suggested that she join the first women's group.

With the older women, Irene was the silent member; she
would share her feelings only if specifically called on. As she
began to trust the other group members, she became more active, and when the second group was formed, she quickly took
a leading role. She was the confronting one, actively using the
group to her benefit for learning about her feelings and expressing them. She decided not to mention her husband in the group.
The group was for her, specifically for dealing with the unresolved conflicts about her dead parents and for gaining courage
from the other group members to explore these issues.

Irene was very angry with her mother; she felt that she had never had a mother available to her. Thus she could not see her mother as a person but only as the alcoholic she was. In terms of her father, she was also angry because, as is typical, she blamed him for her mother's drinking. She liked her younger sister but did not want to know anything about her brother.

One of the other women in the group reminded Irene of her mother. In the group sessions, she began to work out some of her repressed feelings. For the first time, she was able to express her anger verbally. As she became aware of herself and her feelings, she also began to remember how much she had actually gotten from her mother. It was this woman who had given her some of the positives she was beginning to discover in herself, especially her ability to organize and a great capacity for caring about people.

The area Irene could not begin to work on yet was her anger toward men. At one time, the therapist suggested bringing two men into the group. Irene refused to accept the idea. She was not ready. Still too angry to deal with men, she needed to work on herself as a woman first.

Irene's husband was drinking more and more. As his condition deteriorated, he was abusing her both physically and mentally. She felt unable to abandon him, but finally he left her. That created the opportunity to reorganize her life, and she developed a small network of friends, an impossible task when she was married and her husband was actively drinking. She began attending Al-Anon sessions again, accepting some of the philosophy of the program as useful. She had good experiences relating to some of the women there; she was meeting people she could trust.

During this period, she had a short affair with one man in his forties and a longer affair with a younger man, proving to herself that she could still function sexually and that she was not the frigid woman she had once thought. But she continued to be very angry, especially at the parents who had "left her."

Irene had never gone back home and had never been to her parents' graves. The group encouraged her to make a trip back, get in touch with her brother, visit her sister, and visit her parents' graves. Eventually Irene did go home, but while visiting her brother, discovered that he was an alcoholic. When Irene came back, she was furious with the entire group, particularly the therapist, because her visit had been so painful for her. She dealt directly with her anger at the therapist in the group. The group had never seen her angry, and some of them were frightened at her drastic loss of control. The therapist, however, encouraged Irene to continue relating her experiences of visiting her parents' graves and of reliving her early years, pointing out that she understood how painful this must have been. With the support of the group and therapist, Irene was able to work through her anger. She had to accept the fact that her parents were dead and that she must now work on a life of her own. Much later, she told of a dream: she was in an Al-Anon meeting and met her mother, who asked, "When are you going to leave me in peace?" Irene took this as a message that she must stop blaming her mother for what was going on with her and start taking responsibility for her own life.

At around this time, another member, Miriam, was meeting with her parents and working through some of her own conflicts with them. The experiences Miriam described in the group helped Irene a lot because she was experiencing similar feelings, fantasizing sessions or contacts with her parents where she could resolve the conflicts she had never worked through with them. Eventually it grew easier for Irene to deal with her conflicts, and she returned home and visited with her brother and sister several times. On one trip she sent the therapist a postcard from Canada, showing a father tiger guarding his mate and cubs.

Physically Irene has grown softer and much more feminine in her appearance. She sports a stylish haircut and wears attactive, sexy clothing. Her confidence has increased. She managed to face her bosses with a demand for the promotion she knew she deserved and got it.

Irene's husband stopped drinking after their separation and has maintained sobriety. Irene keeps in touch with him but never mentioned him in the group. The group was her means of working on herself, her own identity and growth.

Miriam

Like the other married women in this group, Miriam, age thirty, came to therapy originally for marital counseling. The first session was with the couple. Miriam wore a hat and a sheepskin coat that hid her body completely. She was quite overweight. Her husband, a young man, looked very pale and was extremely quiet — a stone face. A chronic alcoholic, he had been sober through AA for a year but otherwise showed marked signs of emotional dysfunction. He was almost impossible to reach, showing no enthusiasm or interest in anything.

They took seats at opposite ends of a long couch. Miriam was depressed and tearful. Her husband just sat. No contact seemed to be made between them, and the therapist could sense no flow in their relationship. This pattern remained unchanged for three or four sessions, the husband not making himself available to changes, and Miriam's depression deepening. Temporary separation was recommended, and the couple agreed.

Like other husbands of the women in the group, John was largely supported by his wife. He was a freelance editor who got work only intermittently. At this point in his life, however, sober but passive, he was probably pleased that somebody else had made this decision for him, and he managed to get a room and move out of the couple's apartment.

Once separated, Miriam turned to her parents for support. Hers was a suburban Jewish family she had come back to very rarely since leaving for college. After the separation, she began visiting often. The parents fussed and took care of her, and she again experienced both emotional and financial support. Her mother took her out to buy clothes, often purchasing the same outfit for herself. Her father slipped her spending money. But very soon Miriam became their go-between, and she noticed how they resorted to talking about and to each other through her, just as they always had. Father would say, "Your mother told me that you told her . . . " Mother would say, "You had better be careful with your father today, because he doesn't feel well." Miriam was falling into her old role of dependent teenager. Away from her parents, she was a competent woman with her own successful business. At home, she was "Mimi" again.

Watching her father, after her experience with an alcoholic husband, Miriam made a discovery. For the first time, she realized that her father was a "functioning alcoholic." As a terrified child who ran to hide when he began to yell and throw things, she had never labeled the problem. Now she realized that those fits of abuse occurred when he had had too much to drink.

A second discovery was to realize that they were keeping her dependent. Her mother became more openly controlling, and her father (who had set her up in her business) was using money to maintain close contact. At that point, she requested a session together with her parents. Three family sessions were held. Miriam was in a hysterical stage, yelling and screaming, telling her parents to let her be independent and at the same time begging for closeness. Her parents could not really listen. They could only see the "crazy" daughter they felt sorry for, who must be controlled for her own good.

But the sessions were important for Miriam not only because she was able to ventilate some of her feelings but also because she began to realize that her parents could not hear her. She began to understand that she must separate from her parents and move beyond her anger as well as her child-role of go-between. Only then would she be able to go back to them as a mature woman and be accepted that way.

She began to work on this in individual sessions, which she paid for with her own money. Her chief concern in these sessions was still her family. She tried to get closer to her sister, Rachel, who suffered from severe asthma, and wanted to bring Rachel in to the therapeutic sessions. Rachel was closely involved with their mother (who, incidentally bore the main responsibility for taking care of Rachel's children), and she decided not to come to sessions, afraid these would upset her. Miriam acquiesced in Rachel's decision, not wanting that responsibility.

One session was held with Miriam and her father. Miriam prepared herself for days, planning to really tell him off, venting years of anger. But in the session, she was astonished to find herself talking to a different person. This was not the harsh father she had always feared. This was a gentle man capable of great warmth, and Miriam was amazed. He had never been able to show this side to his family. The therapist questioned the change: why was he so different? He said his wife overpowered them all, allowing him only one role in his family: the provider.

Miriam never told her father that she had planned to tell him off. It was much more pleasant to get in touch with a side of him she had never seen. After the session, she planned ways she could get to know her father better.

As Miriam became more aware of herself, the therapist suggested that she join the women's group. This would help her integrate her experiences with the experiences of women in similar situations. She agreed and immediately began working in the group on the issues of separating from her parents. Her experiences helped the others, encouraging them to do what she had had to do. In turn, the group was particularly helpful to Miriam in dealing with questions of her own sexuality and feminine role. Miriam felt an intense sense of failure as a woman. To her, a woman's role was to marry, bear children, and take care of husband and children. This was what her mother and sister had done; she was the only woman she knew well for whom marriage had not worked out. Even her successful business seemed another negation of femininity. If she went out with a man, she was careful never to mention her shop lest he think her unwomanly and reject her immediately.

Now in group and individual sessions, Miriam began to gain self-confidence. She began to realize that she could have a successful business and be a woman too. Work and success became a source of real gratification to her.

When the group discussed sexuality, Miriam confided that she felt she had been sexually abused by her husband, especially when he was drinking. She had no experience of pleasant sexual contacts with men, and she was afraid to try. She began to work on this area of her life very slowly. She had a few one-night affairs, trying to learn about herself and to gauge her readiness for relating to men. She also tried diets, diet pills, diet clubs, and Overeaters Anonymous. Through OA she began to lose pounds and finally reached a normal weight. She began to understand why she had been using food: by eating and, as she said, "being fat," she had kept men away from her. She began to study her body in the mirror. Gradually she learned to dress attractively instead of cloaking her body.

Miriam did manage to build enough security to let the feelings she had always pushed away come to the fore. No longer terrified of inadequacy, she was able to enjoy her new capacity for arousal. This was the last brick she needed for the structure she was building. Once this fit into place, she felt ready to terminate treatment.

Rose

Rose, an attractive black woman in her early forties, was the only sober member of an alcoholic family. She was the pillar of her family, the one who took care of everybody. She worked to save money and then "lent" it to everyone. Her mother and siblings were actively drinking; her father was "on the street." As a girl, she had combed the bars to find him and bring him home, but now, she said, she "couldn't care less." Her husband, from whom she had separated, was also an alcoholic. He lived in another city, but Rose managed to keep in touch with him through friends, and she was almost as involved with him as if they were still together, although they had been separated for two years. Rose came to therapy for help in reaching a decision regarding divorce. She thought the final decree would end her involvement with this man.

Rose was functioning well in a very responsible job in a research laboratory. She had been overweight but had managed to trim down through a diet club. When she came to therapy, she was living away from her family, whom she phoned and visited constantly and with whom she was emotionally enmeshed. Intensely involved in a war with her mother, she found it impossible to express her anger at this woman. She had also become actively involved in Al-Anon, a source of support when she separated from her drinking husband. But what she learned she had never applied to her own family. She could see her husband as a sick person and could pull away from him, but she could not do the same with her parents and siblings.

After a few individual sessions, the therapist suggested that Rose join the group, and she agreed. In the first group session, Rose reiterated that she was coming to therapy to deal with her intention to divorce. But then she began to talk about her mother, who was coming to visit her the next day. Rose wanted her mother to be a perfect woman and could not accept her as a person with faults. She either blamed her for what she did or wondered what she was up to. Rose complained that her mother would insist on cooking for her, keep her awake with her snoring, and generally make her life miserable.

The group focused on practical suggestions for the week, urging Rose to do what she could to enjoy her mother's stay. She should make arrangements for going out or simply accept the fact that her mother enjoyed cooking for her, instead of deciding that her mother was trying to keep her a child. Rose was a mature woman. She was to relate to her mother like a mature woman without feeling that she had to run away to defend herself.

Rose listened carefully, apparently quite happy to accept the group and the therapist as authority. Later she said that her mother's visit marked the first time she had been able to understand that her mother was a human being, flawed like all humans, a person who snored. This theme recurred as she continued to perceive her mother's faults as those of a human being instead of a nuisance directed toward her.

One of Rose's main problems was terror of her own anger. Irene's fury after her visit home was very frightening to Rose, who equated expression of anger with loss of control. One day only Irene and Rose attended a session. Irene provoked Rose, and Rose was able to express her anger. When she was finished, she could not believe that she had become angry without turning violent. Coming from an environment where almost every family member was alcoholic and expression of anger tended to be violent, she — the nonalcoholic, the good daughter, the controlled person — had been afraid that if she lost her temper, she might kill someone.

After this confrontation, Rose began to express some feelings toward her parents. The issue of divorce completely set aside, she began to work on resolving her conflicts with her parents. Once she started to perceive her mother as a person, she kept contact by long phone conversations and enjoyable visits. She tried hard to get in touch with her father, who was actively drinking. When he had to be hospitalized for serious complications of alcoholism, she visited him, initiating contacts that continued. She talked with him, telling him where she was in her life. She tried to get close to her brother and sister too, though their drinking made this very difficult.

Rose had many problems sexually. Sexually abused from an early age, she had been taught that sex was dirty. When sex was discussed in the group, she shared her experiences with masturbation but also her intense desire to live with a man so that she could have sex. Most of the men she had relationships with were older white men. She talked about her need to be cared for like a child by these men and how much she had missed being cared for while growing up. Sometimes she would wonder whether she was having incestuous relationships with men who reminded her of her father. As she began to work on understanding her feelings in therapy, she began to understand that she needed a different kind of man — a man who could relate to her as a woman, not as a daughter, and could take care of her in a different way.

At one point Rose developed a backache so serious that she was immobilized for nearly three weeks. No organic cause could be found. Rose confided to the group, very shyly, that she called a spiritual healer. The healer told her that the pain was sent by her mother-in-law, who was upset that Rose had left her son. Rose had gotten out of bed immediately (she was not going to let her mother-in-law do that to her). Rose knew better, she said, than to confide this experience to her colleagues at the lab: "they'd lock me away." But the group did not criticize her. If those were her beliefs, she was entitled to them. To have the group accept her and not make fun of her was an intensely rewarding experience.

The group was useful to Rose as an experience of acceptance. To be able to share openly and to be accepted was extremely important for her. She made great strides in understanding her family and also her current relationships with men. The group's acceptance of her and her beliefs helped her turn her energy to constructive channels and she returned to college to finish her studies.

Ellen

Ellen is an attractive woman who was born in Czechoslovakia just before World War II. Her father deserted her mother shortly after her birth and then was killed. Ellen never heard a good word about men. Her mother was a sour, bitter woman, powerful but loading a lot of reponsibility on her daughter. Ellen felt closer to her grandmother, who was a tender and loving woman. But the environment in which she grew up was rigid. She was punished, corrected, criticized, and constantly told she was not measuring up.

In her late teens, Ellen moved away from home to look for a job in another city. There she got close to a group of lesbians, but she did not involve herself in a gay relationship with anyone. Friends suggested that she come to America, where she found a job and soon married a young man. He was an alcoholic, and in the early stage of her marriage, she was abused sexually and mentally. At the age of twenty-six, she joined Al-Anon and came to the therapist for marriage counseling. After a few months of individual therapy and a very short experience in the first group of older women, she decided to separate from her husband, thinking that that would resolve all of her problems. She stopped therapy, but she kept in touch with the therapist, sometimes calling on the phone when she felt she needed it, and she continued with Al-Anon meetings. At one therapy session, she told the therapist that her divorce had come through and that her husband had left the city.

For the first time in her life she was alone, but she was building a new life, and she told the therapist that she felt quite confident about herself and her capability.

A year later, she called back. This time the problem she

presented was her relationship with her mother across the ocean. Her grandmother had just died, and Ellen felt very responsible for her mother, "left alone in the old country." She was living with her mother's image. She could not enjoy going out, she could not enjoy being free, she could not even buy an outfit without hearing her mother's voice saying how bad and disloyal she was. She felt enormous guilt, both for having left her mother and for having been so foolish as to marry an alcoholic. She had never even dared tell her mother that her husband was an alcoholic, because for Ellen and her family, alcoholism was a shameful thing. Now that she had separated, she was able to work through her experiences with an alcoholic husband, mainly through Al-Anon. The problems with her mother remained, however. I suggested that she join the second group.

The group helped Ellen understand two things. First, the bitterness of her childhood was largely due to the circumstances of wartime Europe. Second, she could not change her mother. She could only accept her, free herself from that relationship to become the person she wanted to be, and deal with her mother as she actually is. The group helped her decide on a visit to her mother, which worked out quite well, due to Ellen's determination not to challenge her mother's values or to allow her mother to challenge hers.

Ellen had developed many serious problems on the job, mainly related to an inability to accept criticism from her colleagues because it conveyed painful images of her mother. Even positive criticism was to be rejected. She would come to the group and relate incidents at the office. The group, enriched by their own experiences, was instrumental in pointing out that she was repeating her behavior with her mother in relating to her colleagues, and Ellen gradually began to recognize this fact.

At first Ellen wept frequently in meetings, usually when talking about her mother. But as she began to accept herself without feeling guilty, the crying lessened. She began to enjoy doing things, accepting the fact that she did not have to tell her mother every detail. Eventually she was able to plan weekend trips to friends in Europe, taking advantage of her job's travel privileges, and to tell her mother about them, simply mentioning that she was not going to get to Czechoslovakia "this time."

Ellen was the most conservative woman in the group, uncomfortable discussing sexual issues. She still does not feel ready to commit herself to any long-term relationship. But she enjoys more casual relationships with men. Though a little overweight and "too busy with other things to bother about it," she dresses well and carries herself attractively. She seems increasingly able to accept herself and her identity.

Joanne

Joanne, age twenty-six, was the youngest woman in the group and the only unmarried member. She came to the therapist originally for individual treatment. She was very depressed and unable to get in touch with her feelings. She had had some superficial relationships with boys while in high school, but she had mostly hung around with her four brothers as "one of the boys." Her mother was an active alcoholic. Her father had left the household. He kept in touch with the mother, checking on her safety, and paid the bills. But little else went on between them.

Joanne looked to the therapist as an authority, but it was almost impossible to break through her silences. Confronted with any problem, she would always agree. "Yes," she would say, "you are right. I have to work on that." And that would be the end of it. The therapist suggested that she join the second group.

Joanne agreed, but for some time she was silent, perhaps terrified, in meetings. It was hard to be sure she was even listening. The therapist tried to bring her in a few times by asking her to discuss the issue in relation to herself, but she could not relate any feelings to herself. One day she asked the therapist not to ask her to participate: the therapist was doing what her mother always did, and she resented it. And that was the end of her expressing any feelings for a while.

The group was very protective of Joanne. They never pushed her or confronted her, but they did make a point of contacting her nonverbally. Eventually, this became a pattern. When an issue arose, one of the women, usually Irene, would smile at Joanne, and Joanne would respond with a very short sentence.

As the group opened up and the other women were able

to share their feelings more openly, Joanne, more in touch with her own pain, became increasingly depressed. The only way she could show this was by crying like a child. Sometimes she tried to speak, but the words would not come out. The therapist had to hug her and help her relax, cry, and recover from these crying stages.

When Miriam recounted her meetings with her parents, Joanne asked for a meeting with her father. She was beginning to get in touch with her anger, but she was still unable to express it. Her father agreed and came for a session. He is the very image of the British major: rigid, unable to show feelings, but always lecturing. He expostulated his outrage that Joanne had lessened contact with him, and he lectured about the proper relationship of daughters to their fathers. Joanne became the little girl being scolded; the only words she managed to get in were, "Yes, you are right." She was very disappointed and told that to the group. They urged her to have a session with her mother.

Joanne felt that this would be of no use because her mother was actively drinking. But she agreed to try. The mother came to the session smelling of liquor, but she was not drunk. Joanne became a completely different person. This time she was the accuser. But the two women could not deal with their repressed feelings; they could only argue about facts related to Mother's drinking. She said plainly that she wanted to drink, was going to drink, and it was her sole business to decide. Joanne got quite angry, but she felt the satisfaction of at least being able to talk to her mother.

The therapist suggested that it would be valuable to see Joanne's role in her parents' relationship. This posed a considerable practical problem. Father would have to drive Mother into the city, and Joanne did not know whether they could be that close for that long a period. Nevertheless, they managed it. Mother looked quite different. She had cut down on her drinking in the interval, had lost weight, and her face was much less swollen. But the session was a repetition of the dyadic sessions. Father lectured, and Joanne agreed to everything he said. She argued about facts with Mother. The therapist did not feel that much was accomplished because Father took control of the session. The surfacing of significant feelings was not allowed.

When Joanne discussed this with the group, they faced her with the reality that her parents probably would not change. She must accept that and begin building a life of her own. She had been trying to get them together again, but this was futile, and playing the good daughter would only keep her from doing anything with her own life.

Joanne and Irene had established a very good rapport. Now Irene was able to confront Joanne about her anger and her difficulty in expressing it. Joanne related a few incidents at work. Her bosses were a man and an alcoholic woman. With the group's support and suggestions, she started to deal with them. She stood up to the man for the first time and confronted the alcoholic woman with the fact that Joanne was having to compensate for her poor performance. Joanne was greatly pleased with these accomplishments. The group began to point out that, in trying to bring her mother and father together, Joanne had kept herself in the middle of a triangle. She was repeating this triangle endlessly with friends and co-workers. Joanne began to learn to extricate herself from the middle, especially with friends.

She had a very difficult time when Irene left the group. She still could not fully express her feelings, and instead she got very angry with the therapist, whom she thought was not doing the job for her. She got involved with a man and began to feel better. But after three months of dating him, she shared with the group her doubts about his drinking pattern. As the group discussed it, it became very clear that he was an alcoholic, though in a functioning stage. Joanne was encouraged to confront him. The only thing she could manage was to call him on the phone and tell him that he must choose between her and drinking. This was the last she heard from him. Again she went through a very painful time, unable to deal with the loss, and angry with the group because she had been forced to realize what was going on.

As the other women in the group began to find what they sought, group meetings were terminated by mutual agreement.

Joanne continued in individual therapy, where some progress was made. She no longer becomes depressed to the point of being unable to function. She is able to feel comfortable with her mother. She talks to her and visits her—a sign that she is detaching from her mother's alcoholism. She completely cut communication with her father, but she keeps in touch with her brothers. She is also exploring the possibility of changing careers, moving out of the helping profession she chose, in her continuing effort to find something for herself besides the role of helper. But it will be some time before she is able to continue without supportive therapy.

A Retrospective

The history of this group was a progression toward self-recognition and self-realization on the part of women whose development was severely handicapped by illness in their families of origin—in most cases, the illness of alcoholism. When they first entered therapy, it seemed that they all saw themselves as appendages to alcoholism. The married women all sought help with their marriages; Joanne came for help with her mother's drinking.

Through working in the group, they began to function as people in their own right. Irene, Miriam, Rose, and Ellen were all in the process of adjusting to separation and divorce. Rose and Ellen had already separated and Miriam had made the decision to do so, so it was easier for them. Significantly, both Miriam and Ellen moved out of their apartments during the process of group therapy. They bought new furniture and decorated new places. Later Irene completely redecorated her apartment. New surroundings symbolized a fresh start for them, as "our place" became "my place." In each case, a sense of autonomous worth began to develop, and these women began to exhibit in their personal lives the competence they had shown in the world of work.

These group members, although mature women, were still involved in many unresolved problems with their parents, many of which were related to one parent's alcoholism. They had to resolve problems of separation from their families of origin. They all in some fashion had to return to their families and work through the never-completed process of growing from daughter into woman.

Finally, they all had to learn that they did have options. All of them were reestablishing in their current lives the patterns of families affected by alcoholism. By confronting each other with what they were doing and by working on their self-actualization, they began to establish human relationships in which they could act as people, not appendages. They dealt with their anger and developed self-esteem. The changes in their lives were reflected in their physical appearances as well as in their attitudes about themselves and others. By the end of treatment, these women who had been overwhelmingly depressed and angry would often leave a meeting giggling over some shared experience instead of weeping in mutual misery and comfort seeking.

I wrote the above in the form of a paper to be presented at a conference. When it was finished, I called each of the group members for an informal follow-up and suggested that we meet once to pick up threads. They were pleased at the suggestion and came to see me and to hear the paper. As I began to read the paper to them, I suddenly became aware that they had seated themselves in the order I had discussed them in the paper. At this follow-up meeting, I learned that Rose and Ellen had not been in touch with the other members of the group since they finished therapy. Miriam, Joanne, and Irene, however, had become "close friends." Actually, they established a "social" relationship in which Irene continued in a leadership role. This became clear a few days later when both Irene and Miriam requested to see me individually for a few sessions. Irene, the more competent and mature woman, was helping Miriam and Joanne understand unresolved conflicts.

14

~~~~~~~~~~

Tailoring
Family Therapy
to Alcoholic Families

When you begin to think about alcohol and its uses and abuses, a whole range of human behavior is encompassed. The use of alcohol is intertwined with many significant emotional events: relaxation, heightening intimacy, and enjoyment. There is the ritual use of alcohol in the Catholic and Jewish religions, and the equally venerable hard-drinking sailor who nevertheless is careful never to take a drink until the sun has sunk below the yardarm. There is the husband and wife who make a point of sitting down together for a quiet cocktail while the children set the table. There is the woman described by Peg Bracken in *I Try to Behave Myself* as having her own personal gauge: with the first drink, "she sees clearly how witty her friends are. On the second, she realizes how witty she is, herself. On the third, when she knows she is beautiful, too, she knows it is time to eat." And as Lillian Hellman observed in her book *Maybe:* "One of the strangest things about heavy drinkers, me among them in those days, is that much that seems clear to you as you drink, in sober periods will never seem clear again, because of course it never was."

Somewhere toward the middle of the spectrum are the many socially accepted behaviors that verge on danger: the three-martini business lunch, so nearly obligatory that it used to be blessed by the Internal Revenue Service; the cup of black coffee widely depended on to counteract the effects of three drinks before dinner; the equation of hard drinking with toughness, with creativity, with an enviable relaxation of conscious control; and the collection of well-known personalities who have "come out" to relate their experiences with alcoholism, perhaps in a desire to help society improve its attitudes. We even see alcoholism advanced by prominent figures as an excuse or explanation for admittedly illegal or immoral acts.

Moving toward the at-risk end of the spectrum, we see the many individuals whose drinking is increasingly out of control. We find the weekend drinker who is beginning to overindulge on the commuter train as well. We find the man who drinks to prove his manhood, who is reaching the point where he can function neither with drinking nor without it. We find women like Anina Giacomelli, the young like Jack O'Brien, and the old like John Collins, who learn the hard way that alcoholism makes no distinctions as to age, sex, race, or creed.

By now, most alcoholics can be accepted as sick people by therapists, family, and friends. They have learned that they can reach out for help and that alcoholics can be helped. But helping individual men and women become sober is not enough if we do not also try to reestablish a new equilibrium with the people who are involved with them. Current methods of bringing about changes in the individual alcoholic are quite advanced, but we still have a long way to go in helping their families change an environment in which everything is structured in response to active drinking in one or more family members.

Family therapists initially had some difficulty accepting that alcoholism is a disease entity and, as such, amenable to psychiatric intervention. Treatment of alcoholism, however, is different from that for other presenting problems. Basically the treatment for the alcoholic member and/or family dependents is geared to support the normal family structure, does not require medications, and usually does not require long-term psychiatric dependency. Thus it is not surprising to find some correlation with and advocacy of the use of AA techniques in family therapy (Elkin, 1984; Treadway, 1989). In any case, family therapists can no longer ignore the powerful community impact of AA and have learned to keep pace with it.

In writing this book, I tried to select cases that showed a variety of people and problems. Some of the therapeutic strategies used were successful, some were not. The alcoholic member varied in different families. In some cases, therapy began with the alcoholic family member; sometimes the point of entry was elsewhere. I was working in different agencies, dealing with different systems of professional people as well as different groups of client families. Many groups are unrepresented in this sampling. But I hope the reader will be able to derive the principles of treatment with alcoholic families, which can then be incorporated into his or her own therapeutic style and the needs of a particular family.

I do want to emphasize: do not forget to treat the alcoholic. And do not take it for granted that it will be easy to reach the alcoholic family. Family systems resist change, however desired change may be. This will test the therapist's strengths and limitations to the utmost.

This book is not a syllabus of family therapy; you are only sharing a therapist's experiences. Many years of study and good supervision are necessary, and I am still learning with each new family I see. I hope this book will awaken professional readers to the need to get the training to work with individual alcoholics as well as with their families. When you look at the individual in the context of the family, you will find your horizons widening to an extent that the mental health field is only beginning to explore.

Unfortunately, the effectiveness of various therapeutic approaches has not yet been studied (Institute of Medicine, 1990). Questions of complementary treatment methods in alcoholism remain open, particularly because of the multiple impacts alcoholism may have on the individual and on the family. It is quite common, for instance, for the existence of alcoholism to be revealed by a nonalcoholic family member seeking help for a problem allegedly unrelated to alcoholism. This might be a child with "school problems" or perhaps a daughter burdened by the additional chores left unattended by an alcoholic mother. What type of family interventions should be used with specific populations and/or problems generated by alcohol abuse are also questions still addressed largely on the clinical level. The goals of family therapy in families with alcoholism go beyond the discontinuance or at least a significant reduction in alcoholic consumption. We seek an improvement in family interrelationships and communication by reestablishing normal intrafamily roles.

When a family affected by alcoholism comes to therapy, therapeutic goals will differ according to each family's circumstances and wishes. Therapeutic strategies must be tailored to the individual family's goals and to the needs and possibilities unique to this particular family group. A few general principles, however, can help guide the therapist as he or she plans goals and methods for the individual family. A consideration of how these relate specifically to the alcoholic family is a useful way of sharpening our theoretical foundation.

Determining the Focus

In most cases, the most important step in reshaping abnormal behavior in the alcoholic family is to reach the individual alcoholic, helping him or her overcome the drinking problem and attain and maintain sobriety. All the resources of individual therapy can be used in this endeavor, including psychotherapy, medical intervention, and/or referral to a therapeutic group such as AA or RR. Any method that seems likely to be helpful in an individual case can be pursued within the context of a family orientation.

Some inpatient rehabilitation programs may also incorporate other significant family members who participate in discussion meetings, group therapy, family counseling, lectures, films, and so on. Comparable outpatient programs are carried out for family members during the outpatient rehabilitation program.

But while the focus is on the individual alcoholic, the therapist must be careful not to reinforce the family assumption that their problem is his drinking. Human beings are trained — and possibly even structured — to think in terms of linear cause and effect. We want to know the cause of a phenomenon — or whom to blame. Most families come to therapy with an identified patient, whatever the presenting problem may be. In alcoholic families, this human tendency is reinforced by the demonstrable underfunctioning of the alcoholic family member. In families where one of the executive members is a chronic alcoholic, the entire family structure may have been created "around" the alcoholic's underfunctioning (Steinglass and others, 1987). In other cases, the adaptation is more recent. But in either case, the family's formulation is the formulation of Mary and Gina Fitzpatrick: "Daddy is the problem. Help him, change him, and we'll be all right."

The actual situation is usually different. In most cases, alcoholism has become part of daily family life. All family members have adapted to the alcoholic's behavior, and many of the patterns that underpin the family structure are built around his drinking. As a result, the normal functioning of the alcoholic family helps maintain drinking patterns.

Therefore the transactional patterns that have formed around the alcoholic's disability must also be a target for change. The family will have to understand that therapy involves changing not only the alcoholic member but also the faulty family organization. A family organization that permits the alcoholic to interact only as a handicapped person can only impede his recovery. The odds are good that this family organization is also hampering the functioning of the "well" family members.

For the sake of simplicity, let us postulate a temporal framework that may not, in fact, exist. The first step is to identify alcoholism as a problem and to plan therapeutic steps toward overcoming alcohol abuse by the affected family member. The second step is to define a therapeutic contract that covers pathogenic family patterns.

Sometimes the first step is easy. Alcoholism is the presenting problem, and therapy has been initiated by the alcoholic seeking help.

In other families, alcoholism is hidden, and some other problem is the trigger that brings the family to therapy, as with the Richardsons. Sometimes the alcoholic herself is the index patient but under another label, as with the Giacomellis. In either case, the therapist has to uncover and confront the family with one member's alcoholism.

Some therapists would focus on the presenting problem,

reasoning that alcoholism may clear up as a result of change in the functioning of the family. In my experience, however, alcoholism is such a serious illness and its impact on the family is so great that little can be accomplished unless alcoholism is part of the therapeutic contract. This is particularly so when alcoholism is chronic in one of the executive family members. In some families with hidden alcoholism, however, the therapist does have to work with the presenting problem until a relationship of trust and hope has been established. At this point the contract becomes like that reached with families where alcoholism is the presenting problem: (1) focus on helping the alcoholic stop the drinking, making him responsible for it, and by doing so removing alcoholism from its central place in the family; (2) at the same time, target for change those family transactional patterns that are trapping all family members in growth-curtailing roles; and (3) stimulate individual growth of family members that is not based on the family disability created by alcoholism.

In some families, the therapist enters the family only after a long period of sobriety and sees old patterns still governing the family interaction. Even here we have to deal with the alcoholism because it is still part of the family life. This may be because the sobered alcoholic is overly involved with AA or because the nonalcoholic spouse is overly involved with Al-Anon and they never integrated individual growth into family life. As with the Harrison and Williams families, the inertia of the family system has maintained patterns associated with the drinking years.

In any case, the focus is always the individual in his or her environment. Once a therapist has learned to think in systems terms, any other focus is recognized as incomplete. This is true even when a contract for family treatment is impossible, as with the O'Briens and the McCarthys. Individual treatment helped Jack O'Brien and Lisa McCarthy vis-à-vis their families, helping them escape from the roles they had been carrying out.

Family Assessment

Therapy with alcoholic families will generally involve an assessment of three areas (again this is imposing a time frame that may not exist). The therapist must be aware of the stage of alcoholism, the stage of family development, and any cultural factors important for this particular family.

The stage of alcoholism will usually be analyzed by getting a good history and by observation. It will often be important to correlate this with the family's developmental stages. The older Giacomelli boys, for instance, escaped much of the impact of Anina's alcoholism. By the time her drinking became a problem, they were already separating from their mother in age-appropriate fashion.

Many families with a functional alcoholic are already in therapy, and these families are generally easier to restructure. Drinking can be dealt with on an outpatient basis, and it will be easier to move the alcoholic back into a more functional role within the family. Advanced alcoholism must be dealt with more drastically—with hospitalization, rehabilitation, and so on, and work with that family will reveal a much more developed alcoholic family pathology.

The use of alcohol is so pervasive and so accepted in our culture that the therapist will often run into a "how many times is normal" dilemma in assessing the role of alcohol in a family. In some families, quite heavy drinking is accepted as the norm. Some wives simply expect their husbands to stop by the bar on payday, arriving home late but relaxed. "All men drink—so what?" Sometimes, however, a therapist picks up warning signs of trouble that the family is not yet articulating. "He spends the whole afternoon watching football" may translate as, "I'm alone all week because he's at work, and on the weekends I'm still alone because he's dozing off in front of the television after four beers." Children may complain that Dad never helps them with their homework anymore, which may translate as, "Every evening after dinner he goes off to the den to watch TV, next to his well-stocked executive's portable bar." Sometimes a therapist can pick up signs of inappropriate compensation—the mother gives the children money to go to the movies every Saturday because Father is not going to be available for family activities. "We never take trips anymore . . ."; "He always used to help with the groceries . . ."; "He's usually late for dinner these days . . .":

all may indicate that the normal problems of families are becoming exacerbated by worsening problem drinking.

The stage of family development can be analyzed by any of several systems. Minuchin's system (1974) is particularly useful in pinpointing areas of therapeutic concern. With the Harrison family, for instance, the family developmental stage dictated the concentration on the spouse subsystem. The children were growing up and leaving home; in fact, it was Clara's perception of the need to rebuild the spouse subsystem that brought the Harrisons into therapy.

Often, the idea of stages can help delineate areas for repair. Alcoholic families in general have some "griefwork" to do. They have a sense of loss, especially when they compare themselves with the idealized American family, with its husband, wife, and 2.2 children, eternally problem-free and happy. They often have to be encouraged to build on what they have without dwelling on what they missed in the past.

Freddie Harrison, at the age of nineteen, had barely known his father. Becoming aware of this through therapy, Fred was able to move toward his son, forming a new subsystem within the family which let the men relate to each other without the intermediation of Clara or Mary. No "turning the clock back" was possible. Fred was able to talk with Freddie only because he was able to accept his son as an adult. But the realization that his son still needed his father and could be reached now, in the present, was important for both of them.

In a few cases, it may be possible to turn back the clock. Audrey's mother was an alcoholic for years. Audrey took on the duties of parental child, rearing her younger sister, taking on the cooking, and ultimately managing to graduate from college with high honors while carrying most of the responsibility for the household. During Audrey's junior and senior years in college, her mother committed herself to stop drinking and succeeded. Seeing the family in exploratory sessions, I recognized the familiar pseudomature, overachieving, parental child pattern and encouraged Audrey, now age twenty-two, to "take a year off." Instead of accepting the high-pressure job she had been offered, Audrey bought a car and began a trip across the country, something she had always wanted to do. Taking an apartment of her own, she began to experiment with a variety of boyfriends, refusing to become serious about anyone while she was having her fling.

Taking off on an impulse trip, she found herself marooned in another city. She called me collect to ask what she should do. Recognizing the signs of an adolescent fling, I told her to call her mother. Audrey did, and her mother wired the money for gas to get her home.

Audrey stayed with her mother for a week, while her mother cooked for her, did her laundry, scolded her, and in general made a fuss over her, something she had never done during Audrey's childhood. In effect, Audrey was able to be a teenager at the age of twenty-two, giving herself a vacation from the constraints of her real adolescent years. She was able to experience herself as a daughter and a teenager instead of as a responsible adult. Soon she was able to begin relating to her mother as one adult to another adult.

The idea of family stages is useful in therapy but within certain limits. It is tempting to follow the paradigm too closely, letting one's thinking start with the spouse unit and then move to the parental team. I think now that an exaggerated focus on the spouse unit caused me to underattend to Carmela Giacomelli. Family circumstances, too, make generalization difficult. It is not always possible to start with the spouse unit. The Williamses and the Stewarts were able to relate to each other only as parents. It took many weeks of concentration on parental issues before they could begin to think of dealing with matters of spouse intimacy.

The third major area of family assessment is the cultural background, which may well dictate goals and techniques foreign to the therapist's own experience. For example, one of the premises of Minuchin's family developmental model (1981) is the importance of delineating the boundaries protecting the spouse unit from the extended family. With the Fitzpatricks, however, a couple of Irish and Italian backgrounds, helping them relate more closely with each family of origin was a vital factor in improving the spouse relationship.

Cultural shame was one of Sarah and Shlomo's worst problems (Dulfano, 1980). Brought up to believe the myth that Jewish culture somehow protects from the dangers of alcoholism, Sarah made heroic efforts to keep Shlomo's "affliction" a secret from their extended family and friends, while continually nagging Shlomo to "do something about it."

When she was thirty-six, Sarah came to me for help in coping with her alcoholic husband and rearing their daughter, Rachel, age fourteen. She warned me that Shlomo would never hear of coming to therapy. He simply refused to accept having a problem with drinking. How could a Jew be an alcoholic? I began to work with Sarah and Rachel, helping them accept that alcoholism can affect even devout Jews; I encouraged them to concentrate on their own interests and growth and to detach from Shlomo's drinking. A few months after the initiation of therapy, I got a phone call from Shlomo: he wanted to see me. We discussed his drinking problem, and he said, with a good deal of anger, that he had to come to see me because for the first time he was "feeling guilty" about his drinking. Because Sarah had stopped nagging him about it, he had no one but himself to blame for it. The changes Sarah brought into the family made him feel responsible for his drinking and ready to enter therapy. He learned to accept alcoholism as an illness. The most difficult issue to be dealt with in the future would be explaining why he could not drink wine during the Passover Seder.

Interventive Techniques

I have tried in this book to apply known theoretical principles of family therapy (Minuchin, 1978, 1981; Haley, 1968, 1976) to families with alcoholism. As with matters of family assessment, no certain applications of intervention techniques are specific to families with alcoholism.

The process of entering the family milieu may be a critical determinant of success. In structural family therapy, for instance, Minuchin uses the concept of accommodation to describe the way the therapist introduces himself into the family system (Minuchin, 1974). By this technique, the therapist first attempts to gain the confidence of the family members, put them at ease, and accept what they have to offer. At a later stage, he may "join" the family by the use of dramatic and even confrontational approaches.

Joining is developing the fundamental human relationships that make one individual feel validated by another. If clients do not feel valued by the therapist who is trying to change what they are accustomed to, therapy will be impossible.

Every member of an alcoholic family must feel the therapist's acceptance, including the alcoholic. Therefore a therapist must be aware of her own reactions toward heavy drinking. If the therapist cannot accept the concept of alcoholism as an illness, she will not be able to teach the family that concept.

The ability to convey hope is vital to work with alcoholic families. Alcoholic families tend to be depressed and despairing. They have gone through years of struggle, and in their eyes, they have failed. It is difficult for them to believe that anything can really improve. They will come to therapy in the same spirit with which they have done everything else — to help the alcoholic. But they will not really believe that life can be better for them unless the therapist is able to convey that hope.

The therapist must also be respectful of the family. I am always wary of fitting every family into a mold. I recommend an initial therapeutic contract that calls for at least two, and better, three sessions. During these sessions, I keep a low profile, trying to let the family do its thing and through it learning about this family. It is important to convey hope and to establish oneself as the leader. But it is more important to see how these particular people think and interact.

A therapist must be on guard, too, against her own biases — on alcohol and other issues in life. A woman whose ambitions in life are centered around the role of the perfect housewife will probably conflict with those of a female mental health professional. But if that is the woman's goal, as with Anina Giacomelli, the therapist should respect it.

Techniques of changing an alcoholic family nearly always involve restructuring boundaries to allow the alcoholic back in. We do it by rebuilding the spouse subsystem and the parental subsystem, making room for the alcoholic, and helping provide compensation for whatever family members are displaced by the new arrangement.

We help people move into new positions, but while doing that, we have to be careful. Where there has been a parental child, for instance, therapy will usually involve freeing that child from inappropriate responsibilities. But a parental child is not ipso facto at risk. It is often appropriate to get the family working as a team rather than appointing one parent the slave.

Diana is in her second year of sobriety. Deserted by her husband, an active alcoholic, she moved in with another man, also an alcoholic, who comes and goes. Diana's children are ages fifteen, twelve, and ten. She also has a small daughter by her lover and is again pregnant.

The fifteen-year-old functions as a substitute father, but all the children have clearly defined roles in the household. The twelve-year-old is responsible for the laundry and for taking out the garbage. The ten-year-old helps in the kitchen, and the three-year-old sets the table. A group of young professionals watching this family during a session reacted strongly against this arrangement. They felt the mother should be doing the housework, leaving the children free. But the two women in the group who actually were working mothers reacted just as strongly. Diana could not handle everything alone. The children's roles were well defined, giving them the freedom to pursue their own interests, while helping out with family chores. Therapists should always be cautious about imposing their own values, particularly when dealing with life problems they have not themselves experienced.

Even the family paradigm does not always hold—families differ widely, and so does what is best in a given case. In the Dougherty family, the index patient was the father, Terry, age sixty, who had been hospitalized for serious depression. During treatment with the family, we discovered his alcoholism. Terry shared a room with the oldest of his five sons. One of the mother's complaints was her fear that the father would "harm" Francis while intoxicated; she wanted Terry to move out of "Francis's room." But this arrangement had continued for ten years with no sign of violence from the father. Besides, it seemed that Francis felt very close to his father and that this relationship with his son was one of Terry's few cherished relationships. Francis wanted to continue sharing a room with his father, but he did not feel free to say so. He feared retaliation from his mother, the strong figure in the family and the family controller. Only after several discussions was Francis able to express support for his father against his mother, enabling a helpful discussion by all the children of how much they wished Terry could be more a part of their lives.

The paradigm's dictates — to strengthen the boundary between father and son as a strategy for increasing the intimacy of the spouses — would have been inappropriate in this case, which had little prospect of building marital intimacy. In the Dougherty case, the proper focus was working with Terry on his drinking problem and working with the parents to increase their effectiveness as a parental team, particularly helping Terry get closer to his children and helping Meghan deal with the children in a less punitive fashion.

One of Anina Giacomelli's problems was her failure to fulfill the role of a woman in a patriarchal Italian-American family. The appropriate therapeutic intervention was to help her fill the role she saw as hers rather than work to widen her options, as would be the technique of choice with many women in their late thirties.

It is difficult to overestimate the inertia of a family system. Even the most desired changes do not happen overnight. A period of experimentation and stabilization is always necessary. A wife who has complained for years about having to do all the work will find it extremely difficult to give her recovering husband the space to act as husband and father. This is partly the resentment and distrust that have built up, but it is also partly the fact that everything in the family is organized around her taking the executive roles. When the phone rings, she will answer it. If she is downstairs, a child will automatically yell, "Ma, the phone's ringing." It will be a while before everyone remembers that Dad can now be trusted to answer the phone and even to take a message. In addition, Mother may find it difficult to utilize her free time and energy. She has spent her life taking care of children and house almost single-handedly. Now the children are growing up, and they can help with the housework, along with Dad. What are all the things she once wished she had time to do? Therapy may have to focus on helping Mother find a job or develop a forgotten hobby, just as much as working with Dad to help him maintain sobriety.

When role shifts are necessary, they must be stabilized by new rewards and compensations. We saw similar problems in the Harrison and Williams cases. Clara's coping with Fred's drinking had taken her away from the house, where Mary had taken over. Now Clara wanted to change that, taking on more of what she saw as the role of wife and mother. Mary's compensation was new possibilities for her — attending college full-time instead of only in the evenings. Without some such step, it would have been very difficult for Fred and Clara to move toward each other.

In the Williams case, his parents' increasing intimacy quite literally pushed Bob out of his mother's bed. Janet was able to say, "I need you both," but it was obvious that it would be some time before that perception was assimilated.

In families with recovered alcoholics, like the Harrisons and Williamses, the therapist may pinpoint interaction patterns that relate to the active drinking days. It is a matter of interest to family theoreticians how easily "holdover" patterns can be cleaned up. Often the mildest of interventions are sufficient to spark change. Cognitive interpretations usually have little or no effect on behavior rooted in ongoing structural interactions. Simply pointing out what people are doing has little value. People will agree ad infinitum that they are doing something that should be changed and go right on doing it. But holdover patterns do often yield to mild interventions.

In one couple I worked with, Howard had been sober for three years. Now he was trying earnestly to improve a marital relationship that had deteriorated while he was drinking heavily. Whenever he tried to talk to Karen, however, she reacted with enormous hostility and resentment. Karen was reacting the way she used to when Howard was drinking. Making her look at this behavior while it was happening helped her understand that her behavior of the past was inappropriate now that drinking was not part of interaction. This interpretation encouraged both to work toward the improved relationship they both desired.

Chris comes from a family whose father is an alcoholic, as are most of her uncles. She grew up with a strong sense of anxiety; she never knew whether the family was going to have enough money to satisfy minimal needs. She learned that "men don't give you what you have in life. They are not competent."

Chris married Thom, a young foreigner from a traditional, strongly patriarchal family. Thom's father had always supported his family at a high standard of living. Chris and Thom are both working. Thom wants to save a large proportion of their salaries, but Chris cannot bear this; she wants to get the things she never had, right away. Any initiative Thom takes to build up financial reserves makes Chris feel deprived. A consequence of this behavior: a continuous put-down of Thom, which makes him feel incompetent, unable to fulfill his wife's need.

It took one session to put Chris in touch with the fact that she was organizing her husband according to the image of men she was carrying from her own family of origin. When she became aware of what she was doing, her attitudes modified, and so did her behavior. Realizing that in trying to build together, Thom was trying to provide for her, she was able to join her husband, committing herself to their joint view of future goals.

Jennifer and Gary are a family like the Harrisons in the sense that Gary has already been sober for almost fourteen years. But during the drinking years, Jennifer became used to disciplining the children alone in a way that left no room for Gary. It took a series of therapeutic sessions to give the family an experience of Gary acting as father. As Jennifer made space for him, they reestablished the parental system with the incorporation of a well-functioning adult man. Once the experience was possible, change proceeded rapidly. Excluding Gary was a habit, not a pattern relevant to the present. Family systems have great inertia, but they are also responsive to current input. Working in the present with the present interactions can spark therapeutic change.

For convenience's sake, most of the therapeutic strategies considered in this book have been written around the "normal" American nuclear family. The principles involved, however, are general enough to apply to any family form. Two women pooling their income, sharing an apartment with both sets of children, may need the same help learning to work effectively as a parental team that a husband and wife seek. A couple who have both been married before will have to go about the same tasks of building a spouse relationship as the most inexperienced newlyweds.

The therapist working with alcoholic families will see the whole variety of extended, broken, and blended families, each facing the problems of their particular "family shape," compounded by the problems of alcoholism.

Whatever the family shape, people are still "more human than otherwise." Adults need the support and companionship of other adults. They need their own interests and gratifications. Children need the security of parental discipline to be able to grow and explore. The family is usually the best possible source for meeting these needs.

If problems cannot be met within the family unit, substitutes may have to be found. Individual therapy may have to substitute for parental guidance, as was happening in the Richardson case. Sometimes a multiple family group can be useful in providing surrogate parents and siblings.

The Stephens family entered therapy six months after the father stopped drinking. They stopped after a few sessions, feeling that they could organize the family in the way they both wanted.

A few years later, Linda called me, asking for a session with her two daughters. Mark had left her and was living with another woman. They would be married this summer. Linda was having difficulty coping with the girls, now ages ten and twelve. In his case, therapy focused on helping Mark and Linda develop a relationship in which they could continue to act as the girls' parents. The girls had to begin to accept the father's remarriage and let their stepmother into their lives. An important step was helping Linda conquer her sense of being in competition with Mark's new wife to establish a more secure parental system for the girls.

It seems unnecessary to give many examples of boundary drawing because most of the work described in the case examples focused on this. I want to warn the reader that this important work can seem like the essence of the mundane. Boundary making can easily focus on who is going to take out the garbage — a far cry from the vivid drama of the Oedipal complex and the psychoses and neuroses of individual psychodynamic therapy. But "life is what goes on while you're making plans," and it is work with the mundane events of life that is the stuff of building and repairing families.

Our thinking about the causes and treatment of alcoholism has centered in recent years around family processes, mostly because of previous failures with individual psychotherapeutic techniques. One should keep in mind, however, that the type of intervention does not always have to be the same; it may and indeed should vary from family to family (Siegel and Dulfano, 1974). Family, couple, and individual techniques may be used within a systemic framework, and some combination of these may be useful.

Similar techniques are applied by proponents of group therapy, the Minnesota model primary rehabilitation program, and day treatment for husband and wife (Johnson, 1986). To that we may add the contributions of Al-Anon and family education. The interventions may include individual or joint hospitalization of couples regardless of whether one or both members are addicted (Steinglass, 1976).

The techniques of family intervention developed by the Johnson Institute became a very important tool for motivating many alcoholics into treatment. Gathering together family members and other significant people in the life of the alcoholic, a trained professional helps them face their own frustration and concern. In the past, denial, fears, and guilt kept these people from reaching out. They could not betray a loved one. The intervention process, while preparing to confront the alcoholic member, makes people look at their own involvement and in many cases their lack of understanding of the alcoholic's problems.

A thorough preparation is necessary for the group to change their accusation or judgmental thinking before meeting the alcoholic. The process can take many weeks, but when the group meets with the alcoholic, who was not aware of their sessions up to this point, the process can be very effective. In most of the cases, the alcoholic accepts the suggestions for committing herself or himself to treatment.

In conclusion, a therapist must respect clients. Some people cannot or will not change. All families are hampered in changing — they can at best move only in certain directions. Ideally their therapist will be flexible enough to help an individual family change in whatever direction is best for them.

References

Ablon, J. "Al-Anon Family Group." *American Journal of Psychotherapy*, 1974, *23*, 30–45.

Alcoholics Anonymous ["The Big Book"]. New York: Alcoholics Anonymous World Services, 1955.

Beckman, L. J., and Amaro, H. "Patterns of Women's Use of Alcohol Treatment Agencies." *Alcohol, Health and Research World*, 1984, *9*, 14–25.

Beletsis, S. G., and Brown, S. "A Developmental Framework for Understanding the Adult Children of Alcoholics." *Journal of Addictions and Health*, 1981, *2*, 187–203.

Bepko, C., and others. *The Responsibility Trap*. New York: Free Press, 1985.

Berenson, D. "Alcoholism in the Family System." In P. Guerin Jr. (ed.), *Family Therapy: Theory and Practice*. New York: Gardner Press, 1976.

Black, C. *It Will Never Happen to Me*. Denver: M.A.C., 1982.

Calderone, M. *The Family Book About Sexuality*. New York: Bantam Books, 1983.

Cork, R. M. *The Forgotten Children*. Toronto: Addiction Research Foundation, 1968.

Dulfano, C. "The Impact of Alcoholism in Jewish Family Life." In A. Blaine (ed.), *Alcoholism and the Jewish Community*. New York: Federation of Jewish Philanthropies of New York, 1980.

Elkin, M. *Families Under the Influence*. New York: W.W.Norton, 1984.

Flanzer, J. P. *The Many Faces of Family Violence*. Springfield, Ill.: Thomas, 1982.

Forrest, G. "The Role of Slippage and Adaptation in the Alcoholic Family System." *Family Dynamics of Addiction Quarterly,* 1991, *1,* 31–39.

Goodwin, D. W. "Alcoholism and Heredity", *Archives of General Psychiatry,* 1979, *36,* 57–61.

Goodwin, D. W. *Is Alcoholism Hereditary?* New York: Oxford University Press, 1976.

Goodwin, D. W., and others. "Alcohol Problems in Adoptees Raised Apart from Alcoholic Biological Parents." *Archives of General Psychiatry,* 1973, *28,* 238–243.

Haley, J. *Changing Families — A Family Therapy Reader.* Philadelphia: Gruen & Stratton, 1968.

Haley, J. *Problem Solving Therapy.* San Francisco: Jossey-Bass, 1976.

Helzer, J. E., and others. "The Co-Occurrence of Alcoholism with Other Psychiatric Disorders in the General Population and Its Impact on Treatment." *Journal of Alcohol Studies,* 1988, *49,* 219–224.

Institute of Medicine. *Broadening the Base for Treatment for Alcohol Problems.* Committee Report. Washington, D.C.: National Academy Press, 1990.

Johnson, V. E. *Intervention: How to Help Someone Who Doesn't Want Help.* Minneapolis: Johnson Institute Books, 1986.

Justice, B., and Justice, R. *The Broken Taboo — Sex in the Family.* Philadelphia: Gruen & Stratton, 1969.

Laqueur, H. P. "General System Theory and Multiple Family Therapy." In J. H. Masserman (ed.), *Current Psychiatric Therapies.* Vol. 8. Philadelphia: Gruen & Stratton, 1968.

Minuchin, S. "Family Therapy Techniques or Theory?" In J. H. Masserman (ed.), *Science and Psychoanalysis.* Philadelphia: Gruen and Stratton, 1969.

Minuchin, S. *Families and Family Therapy.* Cambridge, Mass.: Harvard University Press, 1974.

Minuchin, S., and Fishman, H. C. *Family Therapy Techniques.* Cambridge, Mass.: Harvard University Press, 1981.

Minuchin, S., and others. *Psychosomatic Families.* Cambridge, Mass.: Harvard University Press, 1978.

Mulinski, P. "Dual Diagnoses in Alcoholic Clients: Clinical Implications." *Social Casework,* 1989, 333–339.

Potter-Efron, R., and Potter-Efron, P. "Assessment of Codependency with Individuals from Alcoholic and Chemically Dependent Families." *Alcoholism Treatment Quarterly,* 1989, *6,* 37–57.

Schuckit, M. A. "Alcoholism and Other Psychiatric Disorders." *Hospital and Community Psychiatry,* 1983, *34,* 1022–1027.

Seixas, J. S., and Youcha, G. *Children of Alcoholism.* New York: Crown, 1985.

Siegel, L., and Dulfano, C. "Multimodal Psychotherapy." In D. Milman and others, *Group Process Today: Evaluation and Perspective.* Springfield, Ill.: Thomas, 1974.

Steinglass, P. "Experimenting with Family Treatment Approaches to Alcoholism. 1950–1975: A Review." *Family Process,* 1976, *15,* 97–122.

Steinglass, P., and others. *The Alcoholic Family.* New York: Basic Books, 1987.

Treadway, D. *Before It's Too Late.* New York: W.W.Norton, 1989.

Trimpey, J. *The Small Book.* Detroit: Lotus Press, 1989.

Wegscheider, S. *Another Chance: Hope and Health for the Alcoholic Family.* Palo Alto, Calif.: Science & Behavior Books, 1980.

Zimberg, S., and others. *Practical Approaches to Alcoholism Psychotherapy.* (2nd ed.) New York: Plenum, 1985.

Suggested Readings

Ablon, J. "Family Structure and Behaviour in Alcoholism. A Review of the Literature." In B. Kissin and H. Begleiter (eds.), *The Biology of Alcoholism*. Vol. 4. New York: Plenum, 1974.

Ablon, J. "The Significance of Cultural Patterning for the Alcoholic Family." *Family Process*, 1980, *19*, 127–143.

Bacon, S. M. "Excessive Drinking and the Institution of the Family." *Journal of Studies on Alcohol Education*. Yale Summer School of Alcohol Studies, New Haven, 1945.

Bateson, G. "The Cybernetics of 'Self': A Theory of Alcoholism." *Psychiatry*, 1974, *34*, 1–18.

Beckman, L. J. "Treatment Needs of Women Alcoholics." *Alcoholism Treatment*, 1984, *1*, 101–104.

Bowen, M. "Alcoholism Viewed Through Family Systems Theory and Family Psychotherapy." In F. Seixas, and others (eds.), *The Person with Alcoholism*. New York: New York Academy of Sciences, 1974.

Coleman, E. "Family Intimacy and Chemical Abuse: The Connection." *Journal of Psychoactive Drugs*, 1982, *14*, 153–158.

Cohen, P., and Krause, M. S. *Casework with Wives of Alcoholics*. New York: Family Service Association of America, 1971.

Derlega, V. J. and others. *Sharing Intimacy: What We Reveal to Others and Why*. Englewood Cliffs, N.J.: Prentice-Hall, 1975.

Dulfano, C. "Observations on Alcohol Problems Among Immigrants from Puerto Rico." In *Proceedings of Puerto Rican Conference on Human Services*. Washington D.C.: National Coalition of Spanish-speaking Mental Health Organizations, 1975, pp. 103–106.

Dulfano, C. "Family Therapy of Alcoholism." In S. Zimberg and others (eds.), *Practical Approaches to Alcoholism Psychotherapy.* (2nd ed.) New York: Plenum, 1985.

Edwin, J. A., and Fox, R. D. "Family Therapy of Alcoholism." In J. H. Masserman (ed.), *Current Psychiatric Therapies.* Philadelphia: Gruen & Stratton, 1968.

Esser, P. H. "Conjoint Family Therapy with Alcoholics." *British Journal of Addiction,* 1971, *64,* 251–255.

Finlay, D. G. "Effect of Role, Network Pressure on an Alcoholic's Approach to Treatment." *Social Work,* 1966, *11,* 71–77.

Gorad, S. L. "Communication Styles and Interaction of Alcoholics and Their Wives." *Family Process,* 1971, *10,* 475–489.

Jackson, J. K. "The Adjustment of the Family to the Crisis of Alcoholism." *Quarterly Journal of Studies on Alcohol,* 1954, *4,* 562–580.

Johnson, V. E. *I'll Quit Tomorrow.* New York: HarperCollins, 1973.

Justice, B., and Justice, R. *The Abusing Family.* New York: Human Science Press, 1989.

Kaufman, E., and Kaufmann, P. N. *Family Therapy of Drug and Alcohol Abuse.* New York: Gardner Press, 1979.

Maddock, J. W. "Sex in the Family System." In J. W. Maddock and others (eds.), *Human Sexuality and the Family.* New York: Haworth Press, 1983.

Meeks, D., and others. "Family Therapy with the Families of Recovering Alcoholics." *Quarterly Journal of Studies on Alcohol,* 1970, *31,* 339–413.

Paolino, T. J., Jr., and McCrady, B. S. *The Alcoholic Marriage.* Philadelphia: Gruen & Stratton, 1977.

Price, G. M. "Alcoholism Is a Family Illness." *Casework Papers,* 1960. Family Service Association of America (reprint).

Usher, M., and others. "Family Therapy as a Treatment Modality for Alcoholism." *Journal of Studies on Alcohol,* 1980, *41,* 927–938.

Ward, R. F., and others. "The Alcoholic and Its Helpers." *Quarterly Journal of Studies on Alcohol,* 1970, *31,* 684–691.

Wegscheider-Cruse, S. *Choice Making for Co-Dependents, Adult Children and Spirituality Seekers.* Pompano Beach, Fla.: Health Communications, 1983.

Woititz, J. G. *Struggle for Intimacy.* Pompano Beach, Fla.: Health Communications, 1985.

Wolin, S. J., and others. "Disrupted Family Rituals — A Factor In the Intergenerational Transmission of Alcoholism." *Journal of Studies on Alcohol,* 1980, *41,* 199–213.

Wolin, S. J., and others. "Family Rituals and the Recurrence of Alcoholism over Generations." *American Journal of Psychiatry,* 1979, *136,* 589–593.

Index